Saturdays

Anne Huson Bock, RScP

Published by Helen Anne Huson Bock
Ocean Shores, WA
Printed by CreateSpace

Edition 1

Bock, Anne Huson;
  Inspirational; positive; self-help

ISBN-13: 978-1537742878

CONTENTS

Introduction

"Hello Dear Heart, thank you for calling the Gift Line. This is Anne Bock, a licensed Religious Science practitioner at the Seattle Center for Spiritual Living."

Each entry in this collection began with those words, and concluded with "I love you, bye, bye." Each was recorded on a call-in phone line on a Saturday on the Seattle Center for Spiritual Living Gift Line (also called the Inspiration Line, 206-525-GIFT).

Each entry seeks to remind us that Spirit, the Creator by whatever name, is our 24/7 companion, and provides us moment, by moment, with metaphors of that connection.

Saturdays have been grouped arbitrarily by season. Most could apply to any time of year, any day, any circumstance. Some are event specific, and are so noted. Some come with focus clues. In any event, with God, It's always here, always now.

THE G WORD

Holy Spirit, Divine Lord, Allness, Oneness, Jehovah, Krishna, Allah… by whatever name in whatever culture, there is the Over-Arching Creative Presence, Universal Intelligence, the Great One, Life Itself.

The word God as used in these entries is meant to be inclusive, representing That Presence, however personally known to the reader. In all due respect.

This volume is dedicated to That Presence and to Its amazing creation.

CHOICE POINT: JUST A THOUGHT AWAY…

Stop downer thinking; change your life.
Instead of wallowing in strife,
Choose Peace,
Choose Joy,
Choose Faith,
Choose Love.
Let's give ourselves a shove…UP
YUP…
That's the way…
Let's get started NOW…today…
It sure beats worry, anger, fear,
All those thinkings we've held dear
Until now…
WOW…

The Power,
The Wisdom,
The Presence
Of GOD
Is all ways right where we are…
How odd we didn't notice
Until the downer thinking stopped,
And Silence shouted,
Loud and clear:
I Am THAT I Am,
And I Am right here!
INSIGHT

It's too late to wait for yesterday
and today is fleeting fast.
Yet, looking toward tomorrow
makes today too soon the past.
So in this moment…now, now, now,
I grasp Thy hand and run.
Today becomes Infinity:
The playground of The One.

IT'S ABOUT TIME

No matter what went on, or didn't, yesterday, we have today—the day after yesterday—to pick up the pieces, reshuffle the deck and give heartfelt thanks that we're back with a fresh perspective, renewed energy, and more practical experience, insight.

That's how Life goes—one day at a time—but that day is always this day, the only one there is. We can't relive yesterday; we can't prelive tomorrow; we can only do our best today. Now.

We have the choice of continuing to wrestle with circumstances and conditions, or of calling in the reserves, that famous trio, The Three Q's: Omnipotence, Omniscience, and Omnipresence.

In other words, we can take a long, slow, fresh breath and claim the power, the wisdom and the presence of God right where we are. Now.

We can say, "You fly this thing and I'll sit right here in the co-pilot seat," Or, "Speak Lord, Thy servant heareth," or "Be me, live me, show me the way."

We can say, "Thank you God for the continual reminders of Your presence, of your power and wisdom, of your love, compassion, support, inspiration, harmony and delight"

We can give thanks that all is well, and then open our hearts and minds to experience and express that wellness, blessing ourselves and our world. We can be so caught up in gratitude that all else is forgotten; we are lifted up, renewed.

"Weeping may endure for a night," says the psalmist, "but joy cometh in the morning." Well, here it is: The day after yesterday, fresh and free, ready to be lived more fully, more completely than any day yet, and that's a hallelujah.

And then some!

IN DEEPEST GRATITUDE

To Ernest Shurtleff Holmes for exploring and sharing his lifelong love of Truth, and to my children: Keith, Jean, Michael, and grandchildren Gabe, Angela and Scarlett, for perspective.

To Donald L. Bock, whose generosity of heart introduced me to Science of Mind; Joyce Borninkhof, who gifted me with *365 Days of Richer Living,* and to Raymond Charles Barker, who co-authored that volume with Dr. Holmes.

To Bob Calkins, whose knowledge, counsel and expert assistance were vital in every step of producing *Saturdays*; Dana Ericson, who rode shotgun; Jim Hovey, Girt; Pat Fox, Dear Chip; Jim Fox, strength and purpose; Laurie Sorenson, Roots partnering; Gary Schultz, John Broderick and Arlene Stephenson, listening; Arnie Marcus and Jan Viney, nurturing; Claudette Varnardo, guidance; Pete and Betsy Smith, Harriett Walden and the Popovs, Virtues Connection, Seattle; Idabelle Buren Parker, soul sister; Anne Scoones Griffith, life-long friendship; Daniel Ladinsky, Hafiz renderings; Dr. Dan Morgan, clarity, and Dr. Lloyd G. Tupper for saying, "Go for it!"

To ministers Jim Munson, Bob Calkins, Kathianne Lewis, Jackie Allen, Michael

Ingersoll, Deborah Gay, Michael and Vaughan Amore, Margaret Stortz, Peggy Miller; to Harry, Florella and Edie Huson and the whole Huson clan, Mabel Longfellow Ames, Shirley Killion, Pushpa Larsen, Anita Smith, Cici Gurney, MaryAnna Mohrman.

To Denise McDonald for prayer-partnership; Jordan McLeish for steadfast support and firm suggestions; Mary Ann Johnson for unwavering faithfulness; Emma M. S. Hall for strength of purpose and staunchness; Sheri Stephens for Merci Dieu; Jerrie Paul, for honcho-ing the Inspiration Line.

For dessert: Dave Bourne and the entire cast and crew of Ocean Shores and *Food Bank the Musical.*

And, to all you as yet unnamed Dear Hearts who've contributed in countless ways through the years, I propose FIYONA:

Fill In Your Own Name Above,
and know you also are loved, blessed and appreciated. Namaste'

Winter

GO GREAT GOD

Happy New Year!

Happy New You!

Happy sweet, refreshing Life—all encompassing...delighting in every aspect of Its expression as you and me and him and her and them, too.

Delight. A wonderful word, meaning joy, rapture, a high degree of pleasure and enjoyment...and, to take great pleasure in...to take great pleasure in. That's the aspect of delight for us to consider on this first day of this brand new year.

Let us let God delight in us...take pleasure in full expression—at last—no guff from us...no blockages, all systems go. Imagine God at the center of our being, a great searchlight, continuously illuminating our consciousness, seeking a greater scope of expression...more health, harmony, abundance, loving relationships, enjoyable labor, creativity, peace.

Say the word: Go Great God. Have your way with us, finally. At last. We give up whining, pining, resigning ourselves to anything less than good and greater good. Freely, we open the doors and windows of our consciousness to Thy delight.

4

Heady, isn't it...allowing our Creator to fully function through us. What nerve to think we have anything to say about it. Ah, but free will can be a real challenge: We can choose to be grumpy, gloomy, sickly, stuck now because of some limitation we accepted in the past. Or...or...we can choose to let God delight in us, shining Its great light through our every thought, word and deed.

We can start each new day with "Here I am Lord. I no longer stand in your way. Live me, live me, live me."

Are you smiling Dear Heart? Do smile with me.   Smile in love, joy, thanksgiving, and...delight.   Hallelujah.   All is truly well. Happy New Year!

FACING THE TRUTH

If there truly is One Life; if that Life is God, by whatever name; if that Life is good; if that Life is all there is, then it's time we faced up to the Truth of our own being: That the One Life, God the Good, has incarnated as each of us.

We might take a look in the mirror and say "hello" to the Power, the Presence, the Wisdom of the Universe, all got up as us. What an awesome thought…what a magnificent thought…what a beautiful thought. And, perhaps, what a scary thought.

In zillions of tiny ways we may have been holding that Presence, Power and Wisdom prisoner. But no more! It is always a new moment of a new year, and anything, everything is possible.

"Let me out," screams our humanity, our humility, our modesty, our moderation and consideration and purposefulness, and peace, and love. "Let me out."

Where to begin? We might start with a moment of silence honoring world peace. We might continue with many moments honoring the personal peace, the integrity, and yes, the divinity of ourselves and each other. We might smile, lend a helping hand, work off anger, or disappointment, or sorrow with service.

We might trade old ragged habits for some fresh new ideas and practices, such as looking for beauty, or being more grateful, more often for the almost incomprehensible realization that Life Itself is breathing us, whether we acknowledge It or not.

Ask, seek, knock says the Bible, and the Spirit within responds. The poet Rumi puts it this way: "Keep knocking, and the joy inside will eventually look out to see who's there."

Happy New Year, Beloved, Happy New Year. And so It is.

ON THE BEAM

This is about being on the beam, a folksy term that means proceeding well.

It's a noble thought: Proceeding well. As metaphysicians we're all about wellness and wholeness, peace and harmony, keeping our thoughts focused on God, on Good, on Love and the Law, on speaking our word clearly, in faith.

Says Ernest Holmes, "My demonstration is, because I know so deeply that it must be." That is faith, Dear One.

Jesus put it this way, "Pray believing ye have it, and ye shall have it."

"My demonstration is, because I know so deeply that it must be." Repeats Dr. Holmes, adding, "I give thanks that this is so."

Let us enter this new year giving thanks also in the true knowledge that our word, speaking our heart's desire into the law, must demonstrate. Let us climb aboard that beam, that light, and let it live us dispelling all darkness.

Dr. Holmes continues in 365 Days of Richer Living: " Certain of results from scientific prayer, I face the problems of this day with no fear. Within me and acting through me is Divine Intelligence forever producing right decisions and right results. I cannot be hurt, confused nor upset. I am a center in peace, and poise is my only reaction. I have no criticism, no condemnation, no feeling of superiority. I know that He who indwells me also indwells my fellowman. I think straight, I feel love. I am a creative center in a universal Mind. My courage is complete, and my strength is sufficient. I am God's health made manifest. Today, I am on the beam. Today is the best day I have ever known. Today, I give thanks for Truth."

The best day ever...too much to ask? Oh, I think not , Dear Heart. We can let every day be a best day...for when we decree a thing—speak our word—demonstration must follow.

Hooray for the old year, and hooray for this fresh new one, another generous helping of time to live and love and learn, to share and shine, to welcome new and wonder filled adventures.

And in this new year let us speak our word afresh each new morning: Today is the best day I have ever known...and today, and today and ...today.

We can do it! Yes, praise God! We're on the beam!

THIS IS PERFECTLY SERIOUS

Perhaps it's time we took a serious look at the phrase we metaphysicians use so often. You know, those four little words "whole, complete and perfect" that get us labeled magic thinkers.

Here goes. We greet each day with the recognition that All is well—as well as we allow it to be. How well, for instance, would we like it to be?

"Perfect" is a good choice, don't you think? And let's take it out of the redundancy and triteness realm of magic thinking. "Perfect" means different things to different folks: To Webster, its meanings include "excellent or complete,"… "exactly fitting the need in a certain situation or for a certain purpose."

For others "perfect" could mean a simple beautiful day, a smile, a walk, a flower. It could mean relationships in a harmonious blend. It could mean paying the bills of the moment with thanks for those who served us. It could mean landing the right job, or meeting that special person. It could be the peaceful transition of a loved one. It could be a huge or a tiny.

As Ernest Holmes was fond of saying: "There is no great or small to the God that maketh all." And we could add, All is perfect for it is conceived by Divine Mind in love, in law, for the express purpose of expressing Itself as us.

When we recognize that we truly are expressing all we can grasp of God expressing Itself as us, that's wholeness. We are then complete, and our "perfect" is our faith meeting the need of the moment in manifestation.

Whole, complete and perfect. Yep…if that's magic thinking, then hooray for magic. Life is good and very good…perfect actually…and so It is! Hallelujah!

Have a perfect day, Dear One.

TRUTH HAPPENS

This is about accepting, once and for all, the deep, deep, deepest Truth: God is; I am; we are. There's no way around it.

Deeper than any whining, or whinnying, or nay-saying is our innate knowing that we are Spirit in form first and foremost, and therefore, there's no way we can really screw up. It's called True Faith, and that's what we all have, like it or not.

Consider the tantruming child that holds its breath until it passes out. What happens next? It starts to breathe again of course because Life is right there ready to express as soon as the tantrumer is out of the way.

So...Life is always ready to express as soon as we get ourselves out of our own way.

Here's what Religious Science founder Dr. Ernest Holmes has to say in *Richer Living:**

"The unlimited action of the Spirit works through me, and even I cannot hinder Its perfect results. The Divine Processes cannot be altered nor confused by me. The Omnipotence of God cannot be stopped by my will. Its action can be directed, but Its flow will never cease.

"I now direct It into constructive channels that bless and benefit me and my fellowman.

All that God is happens as me. I now assume my rightful place in the Divine Order of life and let Power move through me into beneficent action. I am never a handicap to God. Nothing in me can impede the perfect Mind. Divine Ideas use me as a clear outlet for their completion. Heaven is happening to me at every instant….I place nothing in the path of the Eternal. I fear no evil, for God is with me, and God is what I am. All doors are open; all ideas are coming to me. Today is alive with Truth and the future is secure. I am open and receptive to the Divine Inflow." *

Ahhh…Thank you Father/Mother God for this truly good news. And so It is, Dear Heart. Hallelujah!

*365 Days of Richer Living, 12/10
Science of Mind Publishing, 1953

CHOICE

This is about choice, about awe, wonder, reverence…about taking the larger view and letting our little selves be engulfed in the Great Wholeness…in the blazing sun and the pouring rain…night and day…those elements that have endured since the beginning of time no matter how we, as the human family, have squandered each other.

This is also about hope and peace. It's about love, too…love so great it bounces back with second chance after second chance…new opportunities to learn old lessons, to respect and support each other. Notice that hope always reappears…as the Bible says, "Tears may endure for a night, but joy cometh in the morning."

Well, its morning, figuratively, and there's a whole new day, a whole new year of days, dawning in which to get a grip on what's really important. Just what might that be?

It might be a choice to smile instead of frown, to give thanks that we're alive in this moment, and that means there's still a purpose for us. The purpose needn't appear in ten-foot neon letters, it comes in just the next breath…ah, another moment of choice, an awesome moment of realizing that breath is the evidence of Life Itself living us.

Gibberish? No. Common sense tinged with reverence: There is One Life and It's busy living Itself through the only representatives It has...us! That's awesome and wonderful. We can say "Praise God," and we can mean it from the depths of our being. Then, we can show we mean it by praising God—Spirit, Life, whatever we choose to call It—with every breath. With every peaceful, respectful thought and action.

Tiny Tim didn't begrudge even Ebenezer Scrooge: "God bless us, every one," he said.

Every one. Every one. Hallelujah, and so It is.

BROTHERHOOD

This is about the Holyday Monday, honoring the birthday of Martin Luther King, Jr. It's been half a century since this passionate advocate of peace and non-violence was assassinated.

His words still ring out to inspire us to keep on keeping on in the quest for true brotherhood: "We have flown the air like birds and swum the sea like fishes, but have yet to learn the simple act of walking the earth like brothers."

I remember my mother scraping cake batter into the pans, with me and my two brothers begging, "Save some. Save some." She would slide the pans into the oven and then outline three equal segments in the mixing bowl with her big spoon.

We three then sat, with the bowl lodged carefully between us, and licked with our small spoons, keeping eyes peeled that nobody came over the line into our section.

Somehow that seems especially appropriate now…not the cake batter…but the fairness of dealing with diverse beings, of sharing, of respecting others' rights and borders. We all may not have an old-fashioned mother to define our territory clearly, but we all have a fairness figure that never goes out of style: the Father within, the Father to whom Martin Luther King, Jr., turned and returned dauntlessly with the dream of peace in his heart.

We, too, have dreams of peace, as do our brothers and sisters all around the world. Let us, therefore, sanctify this day and every day by realizing we are all equal in the sight of God...equal in our love for God, for our families, our countries, and... equal in God's love for us. Let us practice true equality today, and every day, by keeping in mind: There is ONE Life, ONE Good that is everywhere present...everywhere   present...everywhere present... without exception.

Equality...Oneness...wholeness...Peace: A Mantra worthy of inscribing on the inside of our eyelids, that we might never lose sight of who we are and what we are here for...no matter where we live, or by what name we call God. Equality, One-ness, wholeness, peace.

Blessings, Dr. King, for your continuing inspiration. And so It is, thank God.

HAPPY BIRTHDAY BOYS

In January, 1887, two Holmes boys were born. One would go on decade after decade to delight and enthrall millions by following up on obscure clues, questioning expert witnesses, and confounding ingenious criminal elements, to bring law and order to society.

The other would go on decade after decade, questioning, unraveling obscure clues, studying expert testimony, seeking always to understand and clarify the great mysteries of the universe, to bring awareness of the perfect order of eternal Love and Law.

The first, Sherlock, brainchild of Sir Arthur Conan Doyle, is now enjoying a resurgence in popularity, being brought up to date as a modern superhero.

The other, Ernest, ninth son of William and Anna Columbia Holmes continues to inspire and instruct through his writings, timeless, revealings of Truth under Law...Cause and Effect...that which does not change. Year after year generations are inspired to seek and to find solutions to their own life mysteries in the simple Truth: There is one life, that life is good, that life is all there is, that life is God by whatever name, that Life is our Life, All Life, Eternal Life, now.

How wonderful is the deep peace of realizing we are all in this together: Criminologist and criminal, sinner and saint, literary icon and a five-foot two-inch cherubic minister who searched until he knew for himself the Eternal Truth espoused by the sages of centuries…One-ness…Law and Order under the great Love of the Creator for Its creation. That would be us, Dear Heart, them too. Hallelujah! Happy birthday Ernest and Sherlock.

LET'S MAKE SOMETHING

Yikes! Here comes March already; spring is on the way, and it's time for us to do something really significant before this new year gets any older…

What say we make something? We could make a mess. We could make a fuss. We could make a scene. We could make a mountain out of a molehill. We could make much ado about nothing.

Any of those might be an appropriate choice at some other time and in some other place, but this is such a precious time and such a precious place here and now…let's celebrate by making a difference. And how do we do that? Same way we do anything worth doing: We let more and more and more of the God within, out.

There's a smile in our soul; let it out. There's a song in our heart; let it out. And those aren't all: There are patience and generosity, understanding and support and helpfulness, cheerfulness and sharing. Let them out. There's courage and forgiveness, decency, modesty, humility and humor. Let them out.

And if those aren't enough, we can always make amends. We can make a significant difference, now.

Religious Science founder Dr. Ernest Holmes, reminds us: "Whatever the mistakes of yesterday may have been, today is a new creation."

Oh, Dear Heart, we are new creatures in this new day, and we are here to make a significant difference, not only for own good, but for the good of all.

And how do we do that? Same way we do anything worth doing. We express new thoughts and actions of brotherhood, sisterhood, peace in a world that works for everyone. We make a difference, Dear Heart. And we thank God for the awareness and opportunity to do so. Hallelujah!

TIME FOR PLAN B

This has got to be about power and light and ease of operation, doesn't it, Dear One, whether the electricity and the traffic are flowing freely in our areas yet, or not.

Oh my! We've been treated to some really big tastes of the wind power and the water power of nature, and many of us are still waiting for the electric power to be restored and our driveways and side streets to melt so our lives can get back to normal.

Interesting phrase that: back to normal. Does that mean back to taking for granted our absolute reliance on externals... on electricity to power our homes and workplaces, to support us in our regular comings and goings?.. on our roads to take us when and where we need to go without spinning our wheels and risking our lives? Take them away, and all of a sudden we get to refigure routines and make lifestyle changes.

Obviously, it's time plan B... could that be B for bellyaching...we've got important things to do, the web to surf, and dates to keep, for Heaven's sake...or could that be B for blessing?

When the power is out and the highways and byways are clogged with snow or aslosh with melt…we may just realize all of a sudden we've been left to our own resources. Ta da! That's the blessing.

Trying times can force us to go within to meet our true power, our true light, our true ease of operation, our patience, courage, creativity, the omnipotence of Spirit ready, willing and able to express as us everywhere, all the time. Right NOW for instance.

Says Ernest Holmes: "The light of Truth is within me and I release It in every thought and feeling… … I know that It is my highest Self, and that I am It right here in my present circumstances. God in me at this moment illuminates my whole consciousness and I am free of all untruth…"

So, there you have it, Dear Heart, Plan B…Bellyaching or Blessing. It works for me! Hallelujah. Praise God. All is well.

NAME CALLING

According to *NEA Today* a publication of the National Education Association, the last week of January has been proclaimed No Name Calling Week.

Heavens, Dear Heart. No Name Calling Week! Are we to suppose prejudice, bigotry, intolerance, egomania and their friends and relations are entitled to free reign the other 51 weeks of the year? And for one week we'll send them packing, and enjoy a little freedom from speech?

It's high time to tell The Truth. Let's call names loud and clear…not only next week but every week. It's time to speak forth the God qualities with which each of us is endowed as brother, sister, parent, offspring, friend, mentor, guide, helper, coach, neighbor, spouse.
How about kind, considerate, gentle, hard-working, even-tempered, cheerful, delightful, inspiring. How about patient, assertive, neat, generous, thoughtful, interesting, understanding, loving.

Ah, loving. That's the key. We love God because God first loved us. It makes great good sense to let that love flow from us to each other…the greater the flow, the greater our understanding of Wholeness/Oneness in every thought, in every word, every week … calling the names of God, of Good, loudly and clearly.

Let us give the searchlight of God's love our unconditional permission to shine from our hearts, to echo from our lips.

Says New Thought Mystic Emma Curtis Hopkins: "The love of understanding is the love that shines out from the center through the chinks made by dropping the former thoughts."

Hmmm… former thoughts*…* those would be the thoughts of separation. Those are thoughts we cannot afford.

Now…thoughts of Unity, Oneness Wholeness, Love. Those are the thoughts we can live with, the last week of January and every week.

Hallelujah, we say. And so It is, as God blesses us, every one, with that great universal love.

GETTING EVEN

What's to be done about getting even, even in the face of overwhelming odds?

The answer might be in just four words: Be still and know.

Stillness may be a challenge, all things considered, but it's possible to achieve with patience and perseverance.

Next, knowing. Knowing what?

Perhaps that science, as phenomenal as its discoveries continue to be, did not create itself, nor did the cosmos create itself. So, be still and know there must be a master intelligence, positive, all wise, all powerful, everywhere present. Here and now, for example.

Could that be the Great One, Wholeness by whatever name in whatever culture? Could the Great One ever be overwhelmed? No. Else it would have been destroyed ages ago in the turmoil of creation.

Does the Great One ever get even? Always. It's the law: Cause and effect. Does It ever strike back randomly, seeking retribution? Never. Its nature is harmony.

Webster devotes more than two inches of tiny print to the word "even." Its various usages include " revenged for a wrong, insult, etc," and "calm, tranquil, serene, placid". Unruffled, so to speak.

Which is preferable: The ego-centered satisfaction of settling the offender's hash verbally or violently...or the profound peace of releasing oneself to rise to a higher level of consciousness, to Up one's thinking?

Who said, "You can't solve a problem at the level of the problem."

Who may have hit the nail, evenly, right on the head, overwhelming odds and all!

Namaste'

GOING GREEN IN THE NEW YEAR

Lettuce remember who we are; lettuce remember what we are here for; and lettuce decide what we are going to do about it before this new year's first month is history.

First: Lettuce remember who we are. Re-member means to put back together, so lettuce put back together what we have learned so far in our quest for meaningful life: There is One Life; that Life is good; that Life is All there is. Ah...now I remember...if that One Life, God, is all there is, then this character each of us calls "me" must be part of It. Ah...Good.

Next, lettuce discover what we are here for. Well, if God, pure Spirit, is the WHO of us, then the WHAT must be to express that...or maybe less daunting, let IT express us. Ah, Good.

Now we're at lettuce decide what to do about it. Well, you might say, if God is expressing Itself as me, what DO I have to do about it? Great question...Lettuce ponder it. Are we just lumps of stuff, or are we thinking, feeling, vital beings, alive with Divine inspiration and intuition? This is no time to be modest...we see lumps of stuff all the time; they are called rocks. We are not rocks.

We have the power to choose. Perhaps at one time way back we even chose to stop being rocks... Lettuce keep making wise choices, letting Spirit, God, the Creator express itself as us in vital dynamic ways: Lettuce speak our word as channels of joy, peace, harmony, abundance, health, and, above all, love and thanksgiving...all those wonderful, sweet door openers, clog busters that sweep through us and our experience, without exception, for the greatest good of all concerned.

Lettuce affirm: Father/Mother God I consciously choose the cleansing flood of Thy Presence to avalanche through this character I call me, now, sweeping away all the rocks of fear, fatigue, confusion and lack, leaving me whole and free, well and successful, warm and wonderful.

And so It is. Hallelujah!

GROUNDHOG DAY

Every February brings another Groundhog Day, the unofficial Science of Mind official CSL holiday, so selected by Dr. Kathianne Lewis on account of conditions... Those conditions being the relationship of sunshine and shadow, darkness and light.

The sun is shining, the birds are singing just as they were earlier this week when the legendary groundhog emerged from his burrow in Pennsylvania, and saw his shadow...at least if he'd been here he'd have seen his shadow. We've all seen shadows recently, darknesses we'd rather not have experienced.

It's a scientific fact: Shadows cannot occur unless there's light. The catch is to turn to that light...the light of universal Truth...so that the shadows are behind us and we are warmed and cheered, comforted by the promise of new beginnings.

Thank God for the ability to choose. If and when we find ourselves engulfed in darkness-- no matter what storms of conditions may be raging—we can choose to turn within and see the light, to feel the Loving Presence, the Sunshine of the Soul.

It goes with the territory of deeply knowing we are expressions of the Great I Am,

Dear Heart, so let's affirm together: I Am gloriously, wonderfully, vibrantly, bountifully expressing God in form; I am lovingly, helpfully, graciously expressing God in action; I am generously, delightfully, faithfully, peacefully expressing God in Truth; I Am that I Am in this human expression.

If that is true of you and me, Dear Heart, it's true of everyone, everyone, everyone. There's no use trying to whomp up possible exceptions. There aren't any. What there is is One Life; that Life is Good; that Life is All there is; that Life is our life now. And so It is and so I am, and so we are One.

The groundhog legend can't dampen Spirit, but it can provide a wonderful illustration of Truth: sunshine banishes shadow every time… Hallelujah…Here comes spring.

WWW.GOD

This is about the Inner Net, the Inner Net Provider, the password, logging on and logging off…

Actor Samuel L. Jackson in an interview once was asked about his spiritual values. Said Jackson: Every morning, for as long as I can remember, I roll out of bed onto my knees. First I thank God for all those close to me, then I branch out in thanksgiving for all the rest.

Rolling out of bed onto one's knees. What a way to start the day. That's logging on for sure.

What is the Inner Net, but Life Itself. The Inner Net provider? Our connection with Spirit. As Ernest Holmes loved to intone: There is one Life…that Life is your life, that life is my life…whole, complete, perfect, omniscient, omnipotent, omnipresent…

High speed? Is instant fast enough?

Virus free? As free as we choose. Said a newsman trying to describe the joy and delight of a people celebrating liberation: No dictator in the world is safe today.

Let's bring that even closer to home…right into our own consciousness—no dictators in the form of "woe is me" thoughts can be safe today either. They must go…to make room for the personal freedom for which our souls, too, hunger. As within, so without.

Thank God for the Inner Net that connects us all...the Oneness...the Wholeness...WWW. G O D. No separation, no power outages. We're already logged on by virtue of realizing All is God and All is well. Logging off? No thanks...we're staying well aware of our connections.

Password? Here I am, Lord, use me this day for Good.

Let our Inner Net connection be our safety net, our safe haven, our security, our guarantee that all is well and we are well.

And with Samuel L. Jackson, literally or figuratively, let us roll out of bed each morning, giving thanks. Hallelujah!

SPIRITUAL SHREWDNESS...SUCH A DEAL

Hey, hey, hey, let's check this out: It deals with staying centered when things around us are spinning off kilter.

Writes Dr. Ernest Holmes in *Richer Living*: "I have spiritual shrewdness to see Good where others see evil."

Ah...spiritual shrewdness...no clipping coupons, no calling 800 numbers, no waiting to see if we've drawn the winning ticket, no hoping to avoid getting schwarped again by someone else's get-rich-quick scheme at our expense. No sir.

We are shrewd. That means we are astute and sharp in practical matters...and, Dear Heart, diving headlong and heart-long into Spirit is about as practical as a person can get. Yes?

What could be more practical than placing our faith in God the Good—by whatever name—that which comforts, inspires, vitalizes, renews and uplifts no matter what is going on around us.

Spiritual shrewdness. That's for us. And, it's free for the choosing here and now.

Continues Dr. Holmes: "Peace is mine today, and no person or situation can confound me. I know that the harmony of heaven is where I am and in all that I do. Poise is my attitude and order is my vision."

Now that's practical. Hooray for spiritual shrewdness. Life is so Good. Thank you Father/Mother God that It is so. And so It is. Hallelujah!

SOUL FOOD

Perhaps you've been where the sun shines every day, gentle breezes blow, and the air is soft and fragrant. Remember taking a deep satisfying breath and actually saying aloud: "ahhh...this feeds my soul. This feeds my soul."

The truth is, it doesn't really matter where we've been or where we are this moment. What matters is how we are—the wholeness and freedom welling up from inside, the soul greeting each day: good morning...good afternoon...good evening...good, good, good.

Does that sound too goody, goody to be true? Try it!

See with God's eyes: see only good; see only love, see only peace, see only perfect supply, forgiveness, harmony, delight, and say...ahhh...this feeds my soul...Yes. This feeds my soul.

No matter where I am, it's how I am that matters, and I am good. I bid farewell to my old year and look forward to my new year: Refreshed, renewed, awake and aware, more open, more loving. I am being fed in every area of my life by the warmth, the light, the gentle movement, the absolutely predictable Presence of Good, God within.

I don't need to be somewhere else. Right where I am is God's country too…without and within. A line from *Richer Living*, presents itself as a candidate for Mantra of the New Year: God made me, and I like his creation.

Happiest New Year yet Dear Heart!

And so It is.

HAPPY HEART DAY

This St. Valentine's Day, how about sending a love note to those very special Ones who have shown, and are yet showing us how to live.

A grandparent, perhaps, who told a shy child, "You have a wonderful smile; don't ever be afraid to use it."

Or, a sibling, friend, neighbor, partner, mentor who was always there for us...until one day they moved on, passed away some say.

And we were devastated. How can we survive without their support, their love, their inspiration, their physical presence?

Truth is: They supported us, not to make us dependent but dependable. Their support guided us toward independence. And in that sense, they are still supporting us. Their words, including "You can do it," "Smile," "Trust," "Go within and you won't ever have to go without," still ring in our ears.

Right through tears of sadness come the strength, love and inspiration, the gladness of unforgettable times...the goofynesses, the privileged sharings.

This is what hearts are for: To stretch; to break open; to keep expanding; to take in and cherish all the specialnesses, and to love, love, love.

Hallelujah!

MERCI, GRACIAS, DANKE, ETC.

Here's a thank you note, addressed to you, Dear Heart:

Thank you for your ready smile and considerate ways. Thank you for your faith in life in general and for your personal share of life in particular.

Thank you for continuously seeking greater understanding and greater demonstrations of the truth you hold to be evidencing greater and greater peace and harmony in the midst of whatever flotsam and jetsam are currently passing in your stream of experience.

Thank you for your good humor: Chuckles and laughter really help lighten the mix; glee is good too, and a bit of singing and dancing, in actual practice, or as the twinkling of your eyes, brightens things up for everyone.

Thank you for always coming down on the positive side, daily helping to tip the balance in favor—as the saying goes—of a world that works for everyone. You light up my life, our life, all life. It's true…believe it.

If you'd like the *official* word from Dr. Ernest Holmes, here it is: "I am letting my mind dwell on joy and happiness, and I am knowing that joy and happiness go out to others."

And know too, Dear Heart, that those "others" are also saying thank you, thank you, thank you. Hallelujah, It is so.

THE GREAT FOUNTAIN OF HAPPY

Got time for a very short trip? How about a visit to the Great Fountain of Happy?

So…the storms are raging. Does it make sense to say, "The storms are raging. I certainly don't have time to visit the Great Fountain of Happy at a time like this…that's for the unrealistic, the magic thinkers, not me."

Question: Storms or no storms, are you happy? Or, are you perhaps thirsty for understanding, strength, health, companionship, support and peace? Then, drink my friend.

The Great Fountain of Happy is no colorful cauldron of Kool Aid…no fool's deception. It is the Great Presence—Life Itself—offering sustenance, support, peace, love…all that you thirst for.

Suppose, instead of the Great Fountain of Happy, It was called The Stage Door Canteen, first aid station, Red Cross coffee and donuts, free flu shots…or simply…H e r e' s H e l p. Would you check it out then?…any old port in a storm, so to speak.

So, the storms rage on generation after generation. How about taking a mental, physical, spiritual five-minute furlough, a brief detour from fear and frenzy into sanity: Dive within into the Great Fountain of Happy.

Just close the eyes, let the shoulders sag, and breathe...in and out...in and out.. Thank you God, Life Spirit...Thank you God, Life, Spirit...I am renewed, revitalized, reminded that all is well and I am a part of the wellness, no matter what storms rage.

And so It continuingly, never-endingly, storms or no storms, is...The Great Fountain of Happy, of deep joy, of goodness, of truth and peace. Believe it, Dear Heart. Live It and let It live you.

STEALING

Stealing…not taking what doesn't belong to us, but allowing our Divine heritage—that which does belong to us—to steal through us, to take us over, to move secretly, gently, quietly, gradually through our experience.

How about wisdom and right action gently stealing through our every thought, gradually replacing old ideas with new; how about health and vitality gently stealing through every organ, action and function of our physical bodies, gently replacing with perfection whatever may seem to be amiss.

How about joy, peace and serenity stealing secretly into our awareness and then, BOO, surprising us with a whole new outlook…Dear Heart, we could use this moment together, right now, to take a deep breath and unlock all the doors and windows of our inner self so that good can come stealing in:

Let us be feeling the stealing in of peace and harmony, of detachment and release, of renewal.

Let us be feeling the gentle eschewal of all that does not belong in our life of loving purpose and satisfaction.

For if we were, after all, created in the image and likeness of God, Spirit, Universal Intelligence Itself, by whatever name…perhaps all we have to do is open our conscious awareness to that Presence, that It may come stealing in.

Ah…oh… here it comes now…gently, easily, wonderfully, peacefully, gratefully…yes, gratefully…for if Spirit created us to express Itself…all we have to do is give It half a chance…leave the doors of our mind unlocked and then, in the silence, know that all good is making Itself at home as us. What say?

Yes. Yes. Yes. Hallelujah!

ACCEPTANCE SPEECHES

Those tuning in the Oscars hear acceptance speeches thanking coworkers, writers, directors, producers, family, friends and mentors—all Spirit in form by whatever name, and even God straight out—for support in roles that challenged, deepened and called on previously unplumbed depths of talent and reserves. Heartfelt thank yous for gifts received.

Of course, each of the nominees had an acceptance speech ready just in case. Heartfelt thank yous for gifts received. Ernest Holmes offers the rest of us some acceptance speech ideas that might well express our own heartfelt thanks for gifts received:

"Today I accept the Divine Promises," writes Ernest, in Richer Living, "...I accept Divine Guidance watching over me...I accept the enveloping presence of the Life that sustains me...I accept the beauty and the peace of this Presence ...I accept happiness, and success...health and wholeness...love and friendship..."

Then Dr. Holmes shares, continuing, "I realize that what rightfully belongs to me as rightfully belongs to everyone else...therefore I promise myself and all others to live as though the Kingdom of God were at hand for all people."

What say, Dear Heart, is that an acceptance speech we can accept? Yes?
Then this moment let's set our sights on accepting our greater good and the greater good of all in the continuing moment of now. Hallelujah, Life is amazing.

OSCAR

Oh boy, here it comes: The annual chance for Hollywood folk to dress up, step out, and hopefully step up to receive the coveted Oscar, proof positive of work well done, of accolades soundly deserved for perfect performances.

Depending somewhat on the length of our teeth, we've pretty much all had numerous opportunities to take parts in tragedies, comedies, blockbuster extravaganzas, and low-budget sleepers, hits and flops. And we've moved on...just as Oscar contenders move on to play new characters. Who will Meryl or Viola or Sandra or Morgan or Tom or George or Denzel be the next time we see them?

More to the point, who will we be? Trick question. We are, every one of us, perfect expressions of Spirit now, and each new moment presents a fresh opportunity to live and love and laugh and learn...to be more forgiving of self and others, more generous, more compassionate, more fair, just and courageous. Healthier, too. We've each got our own unique helping of Life, and it's up to each of us to give thanks for It, grow in consciousness of It, and let It shine through us. Stars all!

      "Be yourself," said Irish author and playwright Oscar Wilde, "Be yourself, everyone else is already taken."   And so It is. Hallelujah!

FOCUS, FOCUS, FOCUS

Good day, Beloved! Did you consider checking out the headlines for your daily dose of Good?

Or, conversely, did you consider NOT checking out the headlines for your daily dose of Good?

These aren't trick questions, but, of course, they are not referring to the headlines in the daily newspapers, radio, TV or on line. They are referring to the headlines in daily affirmation collections such as those in *365 Days of Richer Living,* by Ernest Holmes and his colleague, Raymond Charles Barker.

Focusing on *Richer Living*, imagine skimming the headlines and seeing: "... I Am Cause, Not Effect... I Am Healed of Worry... I Refuse To Be Disturbed...

"Today I Make My Demonstration... I am Divinely Optimistic... All Power Is Mine To Use Today... I Am Determined To Know Truth... My faith In God Is Great... I Control My Thought... I Fear No Evil... There Is Peace In My Soul..."

Any of those teasers catch your eye? That's the purpose of headlines, you know: To capture our attention and suck us in.

Nine times out of ten media headlines focus on disaster, devastation, crime, the probability of bad happening somewhere, sometime soon and, possibly, to us.

Bless their hearts, the media have to have daily subscribers, or listeners, to keep going. And sometimes the allure of their headlines is irresistible: We do get sucked in. But do we really want to subscribe on a daily basis?

Yikes! As the Reverend Dr. Michael Beckwith of Agape International Spiritual Center has remarked: "We weren't dropped behind the lines by accident, you know!"

No, Dear Heart. We are here by Divine appointment to express the Truth of Spiritual Being in thought, word and deed, continuously exploring and expanding our awareness of the One Life, God, being lived as us.

And the map for that exploration and expansion may be found in headlines such as "I Recognize My Identity With Spirit...The Law of Right Action Is Operating In My Life Now...Every Atom Of My Being Is Animated By The Divine Perfection... and...The Spirit Of The Almighty Goes Before Me."

Hallelujah! Life is so good...especially when we keep focused on the headlines of the heart.

STAYING CENTERED

Isn't it wonderful to realize each of us is a center for spiritual living, with the power to express all the good God has to offer: You as you; Me as me.

That's why we don't need to complain, find fault with others, or with ourselves. We are too busy doing what God needs to have done as us: Living each moment in the highest integrity, the greatest joy, love, health and enthusiasm we can muster.

There's no need to worry or fret over yesterday...it's gone. There's no need to worry or fret over tomorrow...believe it or not, tomorrow never comes. True.

The only time we have is the continuously-fresh moment of now, ripe and ready for us to give and to receive...to believe in the highest and best of ourselves because we believe in God; because we feel somehow, deep within, that God believes in us, trusting that we'll use the intelligence, and the integrity of the special gifts with which we've been endowed.

Remember the quotation: "All men are endowed by their Creator with certain inalienable rights, among them the rights to life, liberty and the pursuit of happiness."

Truth be told, we don't have to pursue life, liberty and happiness at all. Quite the opposite. We are Life. Liberty and happiness are our natural state, and when we express the best we know how in each given moment, liberty and happiness rise to the surface.

We may be surprised to find ourselves smiling, a little calm smile, even in the most demanding circumstances: Another problem to solve? Extra patience needed? Flexibility? Courage? Not only called for, but delivered.

When we make a demand on the Universe, the Universe meets our need…often exceeds it. The secret is to remember that the Universe, God by whatever name, is friendly and always available.

No matter what we may see as demanding circumstances, all we need to do is say, "I meet this moment with deep knowing that all is well. All is well. No matter what seems to be amiss, ease and wisdom are mine now. I am a center for spiritual living. All is truly well. Thank you Father/Mother God for so It is. Hallelujah!"

And there you have it, Dear One. Let us stay centered.

TIME TO HIT THE ROAD

Let's jump right into the new year with words of wisdom from *365 Days of Richer Living:*

"The Divine Spirit inhabits eternity, overshadows everything, including human events, indwells our own soul, and is released through our act."

That being true, Dear Heart, this season seems the perfect time for getting our act together and taking it on the road...the road to freedom...to health, harmony, peace, prosperity, joy and delight.

Road trips, in the theatrical sense, began in Shakespeare's time when plagues raging in the cities kept the theaters closed. Actors loaded up their gear on caravans and escaped into the hinterlands to perform at the castle retreats of the royals.

These days plagues appear to be raging in the whole world around us—plagues of virus, violence, lack, intolerance, political bickering and security lapses—threatening us with the contagions of doubt, fear, helplessness and hopelessness.

Ours is not to run for the hills or the countryside, but to turn our consciousness within to the safe haven of our own souls, to turn again to Truth: "The Divine Spirit inhabits eternity, overshadows everything, including human events, indwells our own soul, and is released through our own act."

We need only remember God is Good, everywhere present, all the time…and loves each and every one of us…yes, them too, and those, and him and her… and you and me.

There's our strength; there's our joy; there's our health, prosperity and delight. Deep in our heart and soul we believe this, always as fresh as a tiny baby grasping our extended fingers in its soft, sweet little hands.

Let us act accordingly. As the old-time benediction puts it: "May the words of my mouth and the meditations of my heart be acceptable in Thy sight, oh Lord my strength and my redeemer, and I will dwell in the house of the Lord forever." Now, that's getting It together!

Hallelujah! Happiest New Year, Dear Heart. Richest blessings of love and peace to us all, all, all.

UPNESS

Dr. Fred Vogt, longtime minister at Denver's Mile High Church, wrote a book entitled *Up Your Attitude*. It wasn't a huge book, but it carried the huge message: Upness.

The word "attitude" means thinking, acting or feeling, and it also means position of the body, including standing, sitting, lying and stooping.

Let's start with the body: We could straighten Up; stand Up; sit Up; rise Up; reach Up; lift Up; look Up. No slumping or slouching for us. We give our body the chance to breathe deeply, bringing in plenty of fresh air so we can think, act and feel from a position of strength...the position of Upness.

We let bygones be bygones, not specters waiting around for a chance at recurrent hauntings. Generously, we give them UP. We shape Up; speak Up; clean Up our act—that's a good one: What precisely IS our act? Now there's something to consider: What are we UP to?

Let's make it Up to decency, clarity, forthrightness, service, forgiveness. Let's make it Up to joy, peace, love, harmony and compassion. Let's make it Up to non-violence.

Let' make it Up to gratefulness and thanksgiving. Let's make it Up to deep appreciation of who we are, and what we are here for.

Jesus said, "I have come that they may have life and have it to the full."

The psalmist said: "I will lift Up mine eyes unto the hills from whence cometh my help. My help cometh from the Lord which made the heaven and the earth."

Let us lift Up our eyes and lift Up our hearts to that heaven and that earth, that we don't miss the stars, the rain, the rainbow, the glorious sunrises and sunsets, the clouds and the clearings.

Let us step Up each day into a greater conscious awareness of the fullness of Life. And the next time someone greets us with, "Hey, what's up?"

The answer? I am. Thank God. I am. And so It is.

John 10:10; Psalms 121.1,2

WHO NEEDS A CLOCK?

This is about daylight savings time…springing forward, falling back…leaping into the future by the simple act of agreeing to set our clocks ahead and put an hour in the bank, so to speak, where we may retrieve it next fall. The object being to get more light in our lives when it really counts, in the warm, pleasant, growing days of spring and summer. Longer evenings for relaxation, recreation, play.

If we forget to manipulate our timepieces there's the embarrassment or confusion of not being in the right place at the right time. What we really may be forgetting is that we are always in the right place at the right time— never early or late—because we are operating on God's perfect timing…we can't avoid it or escape it.

What we can do is cooperate with it. If we really want to reset our clocks we might choose to get up a few minutes earlier than usual to allow for peaceful meditative entry to our day,..oops…did I say "Our day?" Wrong! It's God's day, and the Spirit within is ready and willing to be cooperative, cheerful, honest, fair, delighted, appreciative of beauty, loving, reliable, compassionate and supportive…ready to produce miracles of good of all sorts.

So, we spring forward into true expression, unleashing Spirit within, out. And we don't have to wait until September to fall back either. We can fall back onto or into the power and wisdom of God anytime we choose. Never late.

And, believe it or not, there's always plenty of light, no matter what the hour or season, no matter what is going on around us, because the light is within. It's a given. It is a given in the midst of peace and plenty; it's a given in the midst of chaos and calamity.

God is God in tsunami, in tranquility, in universal all-inclusive Truth. In thanksgiving, we set our hearts and minds on Oneness…not "someness" but Allness and we are enlightened, and a blessing to our brothers and sisters… to the world. And so It is. Thank God. Hallelujah.

Spring

AD INFINITUM

There is One Life; that Life is God/Spirit/Creator by whatever name; that Life is our life now...Yours and mine Dear Heart, and everyone—that's Every One—else's. And, that Life is good.

It sounds so simple, doesn't it...tripping nimbly, glibly almost, off the tongue. But we know sometimes breathing it deeply into the heart may be a different matter...

When conditions and effects are staring us in the face in the newspapers and magazines, and blaring in our eyes and ears on TV and radio and the internet, we may forget to remember that we are created in the image and likeness of the Almighty, whose pleasure it is to give us the kingdom. We may forget momentarily that God's omnipotence, omniscience and omnipresence absolutely trump all else.

So...what to do? Good Question. We might just step outside literally and figuratively, and let our senses drink in the richness all around us...the deepness of the evergreens a perfect foil for the whites, the pinks, the reds, the violets, the yellows, the brilliance of the new chartreuse greens...the flash of a bird's wing, the trill of a bird's song...the blatant mewing of the gulls as they sail overhead… awesome… awesome… awesome…

And every second or even nano-second that we lose our little selves in that awe, is a speck of conscious awareness of our Godness…soul food.

Those trees, those blossoms, those gulls are going to do their thing this moment, no matter what is going on around them. They can't help themselves…it's their nature.

Yes, it's their nature, just as it's our nature to stand our tallest, breathe our deepest, and say: Hey, wait a minute. Not so fast …distractions and disturbances. This is the day the Lord has made; let us rejoice and be glad in it; let us let the God within, out.

How? With friendly smiles, encouraging words, generous actions, compassion, forgiveness, release, good cheer, and gratitude… lots and lots of gratitude.

Salute the beauty: the trees, flowers, birds…sun, rain and wind too…Namaste'…the God in me salutes the God in you.

This is a life work of course—no matter what the season—because it's all God, all good, everywhere, all the time. God, the One, constant, changeless amid constant change.

God is, Life is, we are. Whew, what a relief. There really *is* nothing to fear. All really is well. And so It is. Hallelujah!

MARATHON

This is about seven days in mid-April, 2013, a week of Life, death, exhilaration, transition, cowardice, courage, cooperation, resolution…Oneness.

Oneness doesn't mean we can just say, Om! Nothing happened. It means we can grieve, we can mourn, and through it all—operative word "through"—we have another opportunity to realize there is One Life, everywhere, all ways present.

The Richer Living affirmation for Monday, April 15, was: I am impelled to count my blessings and to see God everywhere. The affirmation for Friday, April 19 was: Wholeness is my real satisfaction. I am happy with a permanent happiness.

That's what permanent happiness means, Beloved, it means tears may endure for the night, but joy cometh in the morning…underneath are the everlasting arms. In the words of eight-year-old Martin Richard it means no more hurting people. Peace. Underneath are the everlasting arms. And we know it. We know it. Knowing is good. Martin Richard knew: No more hurting people. Peace.

Martin was waiting at the finish line for his Father. Aren't we all. And we know it. Underneath are the everlasting arms. Thank you God, Sweet, Sweet Spirit that It is so. And so It is. Hallelujah.

NOBLE THOUGHT...N0BLE ACTION

Engulfed in this glorious bursting, blooming rebirthing of nature called spring, we may find ourselves caught up in gratitude...gratitude for beauty, gratitude for joy, gratitude for those who have given their lives that we may have life more abundant, more free, more peaceful, more loving.

We may honor the great Master Jesus of Nazareth and revere our awareness of the Christ consciousness within. We may honor Mohandas Gandhi, the Great Soul, Dr. Martin Luther King, Jr., and all martyrs and mentors to freedom, love and peace, in all ages and all countries.

That's a fine thought, a noble thought even, Ernest Holmes might say. Now, how about some noble action to show we really understand and appreciate those who've so sacrificed for us? Could there be a nobler action than freeing our hostages of resentment, envy, fear, prejudice, debilitating habit, procrastination and whatever unwholesome else we have locked up in the dim, dark dungeons of our little ego minds?

Just imagine our smiles of relief erupting spontaneously as those outmoded attitudes are released to nothingness and we finally recognize our Oneness with those of our brothers and sisters we've also been holding hostage as responsible for our griefs and shortcomings.

In one form or another the goodness of God just keeps insisting on embracing us…and who are we to resist? Jesus didn't; the Mahatma didn't; Martin didn't. So who are we to resist our good even one second longer?

With grateful hearts let us roll away the stones of separation from the tomb of our subconscious and rise triumphant. The Bible says on Easter morning the angel of the Lord came and rolled back the stone from the door of Jesus' tomb, and sat upon it. I bet that angel was smiling, what do you think! Hallelujah, Dear Heart. It's a new day and we're free to live it. Thank you Father/Mother God that It is so, and so It is.

MISTAKEN IDENTITY

The Bible, Genesis, chapter 1, verse 27, says: "So God created man in his own image. In the image of God created He him. Male and female created He them..."

Notice, it does not say "Man created God in man's own image." Yet more often than we realize, we may be doing just that...conferring on God indifference, discrimination, favoritism, forgetfulness, retribution, vengeance, capriciousness...all manner of pettinesses we may have picked up through our dealings and relationships with each other.

It's sort of like saying: "Okay, if I don't get what I want when I want it, I'm going to call You names. So there. And furthermore I'm going to turn my back and stomp away and wallow in woe. That'll fix You!"

Sooner or later we may begin to realize God doesn't need fixing...just accepting.

Says Religious Science founder Ernest Holmes: "There is one Life. That Life is Good. That Life is my life now...whole, complete and perfect"

We can turn our backs on that perfection if we want to...we were so generously gifted with free will...or, we can fling our arms, hearts and minds wide open and receive the good news reported in Genesis: 1:27 "So God created man in His own image. In the image of God created He him. Male and female created He them", and in the following verse, Genesis 1:28 "...and God blessed them..."

At every level of our earthly being and experience we can trust that blessing, trust the wonder, the magnificence, the mystery...trust that the Omnipotent, Omniscient and everywhere present all the time Creator is perfectly capable of living Its Life as us, and is waiting patiently (As Emerson wrote: resting in smiling repose) waiting patiently for us to give up our mistakes about Its identity and our own.

Whew! What a relief. What a blessing! Hallelujah!

PERMANENT WEIGHT LOSS

Want to share the secret to permanent weight loss? Give up the extra weight, the burden, the heaviness. Just give it UP. That's capital UP.

We might just throw up our arms and say, "I cast off the burden of loneliness, lack of supply, fear. I withdraw support from criticism, jealousy, sarcasm. I no longer have room for grief, or woe, or worry.

"They weigh me down. They darken each day. They are too heavy to bear any longer. And, I no longer have room for bigotry, or righteous indignation or immodesty or contempt, or intolerance, or indecency.

"Out! Out! Out!"

Truly, aren't you starting to feel lighter already? This is a diet of Self determination: Fasting from the promptings of ego. Poor ego, it thinks it has to fight for its share, to get there first, to be better than someone else, to protect, defend, outmaneuver. Poor ego...here, have a cookie.

To whom are we being disloyal if we refuse to let go of the heaviness of grief for a departed loved one...or the horrendous load of guilt from a so-called failure or REALLY SIGNIFICANT MISTAKE, or the shoulder slumping memory of having been *victimized,* or the mountainous boulders enduring through the years from the **great disappointment**?

To whom are we being disloyal if we continue to wrap ourselves in layers of cherished limitation? To the Spirit within, that's to whom. To God Itself, by whatever name. That's to whom!

Oh, when put that way, permanent weight loss takes on new meaning: A lighter heart, a lighter step, a lighter outlook, a lighter you, a lighter me, a lighter us…in every way.

Isn't Life grand! Hallelujah.

SECURITY BLANKETS

Little children are amazing teachers when we pay attention. For one thing, they show the importance—the necessity really—of security blankets.

Try to relieve a tot of his or her blankie for a well-earned laundering, and one is confronted with distraught wailing. Replace the worn out raggy thing with a fine new blankie, and the recipient is inconsolable.

Why? Because children innately sense the wonder, the peace, the pleasure of being wrapped in that which they believe keeps them safe and secure.

So do we. But we don't need to tote around a physical blankie. For us, it's an inside job—the total security of knowing deep, deep, deep in our hearts that we are safe, secure, loved and supported by a power greater than we are—an unassailable power—one that doesn't wear out, or wear thin, or ever need laundering. One that is a constant, reliable source of comfort and inspiration.

Dr. Holmes shares: "What I see as a problem, God sees as an opportunity to release his intelligence. Knowing this, I am confident and serene. Neither a person nor a situation can confound me. I silently turn within and find the spiritual answer…Rejoicing in this perfect supply of inspiration, I cannot fail. Where I am at every moment, His Mind is. This is my security; this is my peace…"

And this, Dear Heart, is a security blanket to top all blankets: God's presence is our security, our peace. It's a wrap for sure. Hallelujah!

Thank you Father/Mother God that this is so, for so It is.

SHAPING UP

"What YOU need is a good talking to." Ever hear those words as a child? And then came the Dutch Uncle bit—so you could prepare yourself to be told the truth involving, of course, how you could shape up.

Webster defines Dutch Uncle as "a person, often a mentor or advisor, who criticizes or reproves with unsparing severity or frankness."

In defining Dutch Uncle, Webster doesn't actually specify gender... just "a person." So conceivably Dutch Uncle could be Dutch Aunt. And just who might fill that role in The Religious Science philosophy? Of course, our mentor and mystic Emma Curtis Hopkins. The perfect choice, and here she is now with some choice words, unsparingly frank about how we can shape up. Ready?

Number One: "The secret of freedom is in knowing what ideas are prejudices and should be dropped out of mind."

Number two: " If you feel all the time as though you ought to be protecting yourself from mankind, either financially or as to reputation, stop and think...if God is your world, what have you to fear?"

Number three: "There is no sin, sickness or death. Where is there no sin, sickness or death? In God, of course. Where is God? Everywhere."

Number Four: "God works through me to will and do that which ought to be done by me. Be sure this is true. It is a great rest to think how many unnecessary things we have been doing that we are now relieved from doing."

And Five: " Don't complain!"

There you have it, Dear Heart. In the Wizard of Oz, Dorothy had her Auntie Em. In Religious Science we have our very own Dutch Aunt Emma. And she tells us how to get home too. Hallelujah.

SHARING THE GOOD

Today we're sharing the Morning Resolve of our Episcopal brothers and sisters from a little devotional booklet called *Forward Day by Day*. Here it is:

"I will try this day to live a simple, sincere and serene life, repelling promptly every thought of discontent, anxiety, discouragement, impurity, and self-seeking; cultivating cheerfulness, magnanimity, charity and the habit of Holy silence; exercising economy in expenditure, generosity in giving, carefulness in conversation, diligence in appointed service, fidelity to every trust, and a childlike faith in God."

That pretty much covers the criteria for a well-balanced day, doesn't it...calling forth the Christ spirit within each of us to full and glorious expression, certainly for the highest good of ourselves and all with whom we come in contact.

What a wonderful treatment, and while we're at it, let's live! So, we goof up on a point or two, maybe our giving is less than generous, or certain words creep into our conversation...if so, we thank God for a moment of increased awareness, and keep going.

And tomorrow we keep going, and the next day and the next, relishing every opportunity to see ourselves more clearly…as God sees us: whole, complete, perfect, and loved, loved, loved, Absolutely. We're not here to earn God's love, but to let it express more and more fully in, through and as each one of us.

Oh, hooray! Life is so good, this day and every day—even the trying ones. Hallelujah!

THE PERFECT CHOICE

Says Religious Science founder Ernest Holmes in *Richer Living,* "I live in the One Mind and act through the One Body, in accord with divine harmony, perfection and poise. Every organ of my body moves in accord with perfect harmony. The Divine circulates through me automatically, spontaneously and perfectly. Every atom of my being is animated by the Divine Perfection."

And, Dear Heart, what is true of our physical body is just as true of our body of affairs, our finances, livelihoods, relationships, every bit and speck of our here and now life expression. All is God. All is Good. Perfection.

We can accept that Truth now, and dwell in it moment by moment, or...we can horse around pretending that lack, limitation and illness are ordained by God for our earthly experience. Doesn't sound like much of a choice to me. What do you think?

Great! Perfection it is, then, and with grateful hearts we can join in one enthusiastic Hallelujah!

And so It is.

THE QUESTION and THE ANSWER

Religious Science is about the heart and the wonders it experiences when it turns from outward limitations, confusion and fear, to the inward joy, strength and courage of the awareness of One-ness with the Creator.

Sound a bit glib perhaps? "Oh sure…things aren't going too well in my life, think I'll just turn within."

But truly, that is ALL one has to do. It may help to close the eyes, and to ask a simple question: Who am I? Who am I? Who am I? …I must be more than an accidental blip on the radar screen of a transitory life. There must be a reason for my being in this place, in this time. Who am I?

From scripture comes the answer: I am the Christ, the son…or daughter… of the Living God. Here that God may express more fully NOW by means of me. Here that I may know that which has created me in the image and likeness of Itself. Here that I may know, for sure, that I am never, ever alone.

Says Dr. Holmes, "God is my companion. It is impossible for me to be lonely or alone, for wherever I go the One Presence will accompany me. … I have a partnership with the Infinite which is steady and strong and certain.

This same Presence I feel in everyone else—the One Companion of all.

"I am guided by this Presence, I am guarded by It, I am kept in the shadow of Its strength. I am fed by the bounty of Its love. I am guided by Its wisdom. ... In this companionship there is love and beauty, there is peace and joy, there is happiness and success, today and forever more."

Who am I? Good question. God's companion. Good answer.

Hallelujah and so It is!

GRUMPY TULIP, ANYONE?

Spring showers! Ah, how refreshing. How delighted the bulbs must be to feel their helping of life bursting out and up and into full expression to the glory of God.

Do the fresh flower shoots carry resentments for the months of darkness from which they are now emerging? Ever see a grumpy tulip? No, they are made fresh and pure and perfect. They don't pick on each other either. Ever see a daffodil slug a crocus?

Where is this going? To the thought of the wonderful spring showers. How about we spring into the spirit of the whole thing ourselves and treat our consciousness to a thorough washing away of any deep down dark dubious thoughts about our relationships with ourselves, our fellow beings and our Creator. Then, freshly showered, we may rise up into the full expression of life without conditions. Oops…fat chance!

There will always be conditions. But… there will always be God/Spirit offering us unconditional love. In amazement and gratitude can we do less than return the favor?

Says Dr. Raymond Charles Barker in *Richer Living*: "The true metaphysician has erased the possibility of seeing evil in his (or her) fellowman, and has gone beyond forgiveness into complete spiritual understanding. This is the forward look. This is the upward reach."

Dr. Barker continues: "I have found God where I formerly believed error to exist. I praise and bless the good of all whom I know. Divine love in me reaches out and enfolds them in understanding and peace. I now am at peace with God and man."

I repeat: Have you ever seen a grumpy tulip, or a daffodil slug a crocus?

Today, Dear Heart, is a new day, and we are made new in it by belief in, and embodiment of Oneness. Oneness...that's when you and I and we and they give up grumpiness and stop slugging one another and realize there's one life, it's good, and we're all in it together. All, all, all...no exceptions.

Thank you Father/Mother God that this is so, for so It surely is! Hallelujah!

TURNING INSIDE OUT

All it takes to be a practitioner of Religious Science is willingness to turn yourself inside out, letting the inborn joy, power, peace, wisdom—the good of God—be revealed in your own experience and in that of all with whom you come in contact.

Doesn't that sound simple? And it is. Simple, not necessarily easy to look less-than-pleasant conditions and effects, seeming lack and limitation straight in the eye and say, "No thank you. There's good for me, and I ought to have it."

"There's good for me, and I ought to have it." That phrase is from Emma Curtis Hopkins. She equated good with God as did Ernest Holmes, who writes in *Richer Living* in part:

"My faith In God is so great that I have no faith in evil…I know God alone is power and is presence. Life to me is an affirmative action of thought. I think affirmatively this day, knowing that good is created, maintained and extended by so doing…God's thoughts are now my thoughts, and good appears instantly wherever I look.

"Recognizing only the one true Source of my thinking, I experience only the one possible effect in my experience—the effect of good.

Controlled, poised and sure, I see God everywhere as I think his thoughts with him."

So, Dear Heart, there is good for us, and we do have it as we willingly practice letting the God, the good within, out and encouraging others to do likewise.

Thank you Father/Mother God for Thy eternal goodness flowing in, through and as us, and for the right, insight and ability to practice the Presence of Good—Thy Presence—in the continuing moment of now.

Hallelujah. So It is!

ROLLING STONES

At Easter time the message of course is about renewal...about realizing that it is within our reach to be made new and fresh again, free and whole. The promise of Easter, the promise of spring is rebirth...new life...resurrection, if you will...and it's just a thought away.

In the Biblical Easter story is this line: "And the angel of the Lord came and rolled back the stone from the door and sat upon it."

And when that stone was rolled away, light flooded the tomb, driving out the darkness, revealing the tomb to be empty, not black and filled with despair.

Our conscious awareness can send an angel—a focused thought—to roll away any stones keeping tombs of darkness bottled up deep inside our subconscious.

New thought pioneer Malinda Cramer explained healings in her life experience this way: "The old conditions passed away as fast as I disowned the old habits of belief."

Does it make sense to keep ourselves in the dark with heavy, stone-ish thoughts like...oh, I couldn't...not now...I'm too tired...too depressed...too sick...too poor...too worthless...too old...too young...(Can you imagine anyone actually being too young?!).

What say we take a moment right now, follow Malinda Cramer's lead and disown heavy old habit thoughts blocking our renewal:

Dearest Father/Mother God, knowing you are all-wise, all-powerful, everywhere present, and ALL there is...including us, thank Heaven...We now declare all blockages to our highest good, all stones guarding secret darknesses in our subconscious to be rolled away, letting lightness flood our being with highest good: health,   harmony,   joy, abundance,   worthwhile   activity,   peace, enthusiasm, new life. Amen.

Yes, Dear Heart. Just feel the tide of relief and gratitude welling up in the beauty of our   very   breath...fresh,   pure,   sweet, wholeness. The angel of the Lord—conscious focused thought—can   roll away any stone, any time, and, if it so chooses...sit upon it, and smile. Hallelujah.

RESURRECTION

St. Matthew, 28.2 KJV:
And, behold, there was a great
earthquake: For the angel of the Lord
descended from Heaven, and came and
rolled back the stone From the door, and
sat upon it.

For many the world over, the traditional Easter morning greeting is "Hallelujah, Christ is risen!" And the response is "Christ is risen indeed!"

How glorious and hope filled. The Bible tells us the angel of the Lord rolled away the stone from the entrance of the tomb where Jesus' body had been placed following the crucifixion. And the tomb was found empty for Christ had risen from the dead...the depths of darkness.

Dear Heart, are not we ourselves angels of the Lord, entrusted with the responsibility of rolling the stone away from the depths of our own hearts...that peace, harmony, beauty and love might escape from their imprisonment and burst forth in the dawn of the new day...to reign supreme in a world sorely in need of that very peace, harmony, beauty and love...in need of brotherhood, the recognition of Oneness under a most uncommon common Creator, God the

Holy, Spirit, the All in All, the One, by whatever name.

In a favorite expression of Dr. Holmes, this might sound pretty "High kaflutin'"...angels of the Lord, indeed!

But what a vivid symbol...rolling away the stone from the door, and then what?...sitting on that stone in satisfaction and release, as Life rushes forth, full and fresh and free.

Can we not be totally, marvelously "high kaflutin" saying "I am *that* I am, and I am reborn whole, complete and perfect...not just on Easter morning once a year, but every morning of every day allotted to us. It's a big job, but somebody has it to do.

The Christ spirit within us longs to burst forth, expressing more good for all than we can even imagine in our finitehood. Can we refuse, letting fear and limitation keep that tombstone lodged firmly in place?

I think not, Dear Heart. What do you think? In all awe and respect for those who bravely coined the phrase...Let's roll!

Hallelujah. So be It.

OPTIONS, OPTIONS, OPTIONS

Options. That word has several meanings, and they all involve choice.

Some folks like to keep all their options open, so they don't have to choose. Some like to choose all the available options, rather like loading up a new car with all possible equipment.

Some let their options lapse, not making a specific choice before the time limit expires, and so being left with the feeling they've missed out.

In football, the back has the option of passing or running with the ball.

Life is full of options, the number one definition of which is the power or right to choose.

The question arises: Are we using our powers, exercising our rights for our highest good (and the highest good of all concerned)?

Dr. Kathianne Lewis says there's really only one option or choice to be made if we want to life fully, largely, gloriously, and that is to choose more God, more God, and yet more God, continually opening to that which promotes positive, beautiful, responsible, joyous living…more God.

Let us open our hearts together this moment, Dear One, really open, so that irritations, glitches, snits, woes, and disappointments drop by the wayside as we plunge deeper and deeper into the awareness that we are Spiritual Beings. As such we always have the power and the right to choose and re-choose health, harmony, abundance, creative expression, soul-satisfying relationships, Divine guidance, and Right Action.

Dr. Kathianne calls it "going toe-to-toe" with God. Jesus said, "I have come that ye may have life, and have it more abundantly."

Let us exercise our options to do just that…to knock, to ask, to seek…more God, ever more God.

So what if the civil authorities can order seasonal switcheroos with our clocks, watches and timetables: Spring forward, fall back, as it were. In Spirit there is no time or space, only the continuing moment of now.

So, in this moment let us say together, "Be me, live me Lord. I choose Life—full out, fresh, new, here, now. Wow!"

And so It is. Hallelujah!

WAITING WORKS BOTH WAYS

One of Emma Curtis Hopkins' many names for God, the Creator, is the Waiting Adequate. What could God possibly be waiting on us for? Perhaps for us to knock, that doors may be opened; perhaps to seek, that we may find; perhaps simply to ask, that our prayers may be answered.

Thank Heaven for Spiritual Mind Treatment lessons teaching us to speak our word clearly and with intention, affirming God's adequacy to provide the health, harmony, right action, peace, love, abundance of good in whatever area our human experience seems to be less than the perfection for which our hearts hunger.

And then what? Often it seems then it's our turn to wait. Well, what if we are waiting? What if we have waited and waited and waited already? What if we've even just added another p.s. to our treatments for patience?

"Wait on the Lord" says the psalmist, "Be of good courage, and (the Lord) shall strengthen thine heart. Wait I say, on the Lord."

Can we wait adequately...that is, fully, sufficiently, capably, continuing to believe our good is manifesting now, soon to appear in form and/or experience?

We can when we plug in our good courage, as the psalmist suggests, and allow our hearts to be strengthened, to feel the wisdom and power and presence of God flowing in, through and as us this moment.

We can pass the time by giving thanks cheerfully, for every bit of good we see, taste, touch, smell and feel. We can even bless the waiting for giving us the opportunity to expand our inner courage; to realize more deeply that God—the Waiting Adequate—is everywhere all the time, and that means here and now.

Should we run out of things to occupy our attention while waiting, we might redo our waiting rooms: open the windows; sweep the floors, and put a bouquet of fresh thoughts, sweet, colorful blossoms of peace, harmony and freedom on the banquet table. Ah…yes…There! That's better! That's much better!

THE BIG THREE

This is about insight, celebration and thanksgiving…all of which show up in this little vignette from the life of Religious Science founder Ernest Holmes. We thank Dr. Holmes' life-long friend Reginald C. Armor* for sharing.

"It was Dr. Holmes custom to close his Mother's Day Sunday service with a dramatic reading of the poem **Mother 'o Mine** by Rudyard Kipling.

Imagine with me, this short stocky man gripping the podium and giving full vent to his love for his own mother, and his love for the dramatic:

> If I were hanged on the highest hill,
> Mother 'o mine, O Mother 'o mine!
> I know whose love would follow me still,
> Mother 'o mine, O Mother 'o mine!

Dr. Holmes' voice would rise to the top of that hill, then sink to the depths of the sea:

> If I were drowned in the deepest sea,
> Mother 'o mine, O Mother 'o mine!
> I know whose tears would come down to me, Mother 'o mine, O Mother 'o mine!

Tears were beginning to well up in the congregation, and to roll unashamedly down Dr. Holmes' cheeks, as he concluded:

If I were damned of body and soul,
Mother 'o mine, O Mother 'o mine!
I know whose prayers would make
me whole, Mother 'o mine,
O Mother 'o mine!

Dr. Holmes would lean on the podium as if for support, reach for his handkerchief, stand for a moment, transfixed, mopping his eyes...then look out at the somber congregation, and say:

'Isn't it terrible to see a fat man cry?'

The mood was broken, smiles reappeared, the Mother's Day celebration had begun, and hearts were light with thanksgiving."

So there it is, Dear Heart: insight, celebration and thanksgiving to inspire us this day, and did I mention humor? Oh yes, humor, so very important, it surely must be among the favorite virtues we were born with, thanks to our beloved Mother/Father God. And so It is. Hallelujah!

*from **Ernest Holmes THE MAN**
(Science of Mind Publications, 1977)

FRONT LINE DUTY

As Memorial Day approaches, we find ourselves thinking of friends and family, loved ones who have gone on ahead. And we may think especially of those in peril in war zones, both past and present.

Ernest and Hazel Holmes had no children of their own, but they gave thousands of copies of *This Thing Called Life* for servicemen and women in the Pacific in World War II.

Judge Thomas Troward, Ernest's mentor, had a son, Rupert, in World War I. Writing to Rupert, who had just been pronounced fit for front line duty, Judge Troward says in part, "My very dear son, your daily prayer should be simply this: Let me find Thee this day in myself, and then go forward in the full confidence that your prayer has been answered. This is not vain repetition, but the highest operation of the Law of Cause and Effect.

"Put your whole trust in Him and fear not," Judge Troward continues, "This does not mean making long prayers...what it does mean is a constant dwelling in thought upon the continual presence of God with us and around us...a sort of constant conversation with God in our heart—nothing too good for Him to do for us and nothing of ours too small for Him to take notice of."

Dear Heart, each moment we face front line duty in our own life challenges, large and small. Always available is the choice to express the highest and best of which we are capable...let me find Thee this day in myself...as compassion, courage, determination, forgiveness, honesty, decency, industry, kindness, flexibility...whatever the situation calls for.

May the Troward prayer be our mantra: Let me find Thee this day in myself...Let me find Thee this day in myself...and then let us go forward in full confidence that our prayer has been answered. In fact, let us go forward not only in full confidence, but in peacefulness, in joy and in thanksgiving.

Rupert? He returned safely from the front lines, and so can we. Praise God.

SURRENDERING TO PEACE

This is about peace...deep, wonderful, ever-available peace.

How fortunate we are to know deep down that God, that Good, prevails; that the love of the Creator for Its creation—us—is deeper than any complaining, or nay-saying on our part; that when we finally quit surrendering to worry, anger, cynicism, hopelessness, etc., and surrender instead to the inner goodness, that goodness has a chance to manifest.

Spirit is so accommodating: It allows us to bad-mouth It, ignore It, and wallow in whatever horrendous catastrophe is of the moment. But...It never gives up on us. Infinite Patience waits; Infinite Love enfolds; Infinite Peace is.

And that's the power that transforms catastrophes, that lets us see good where before we saw misfortune, light where there seemed only darkness.

Are we for world peace? Let us say so. Peace on Earth isn't just a slogan for holiday cards. It's the mantra for holy days of year-long, loving living.

Peace on earth begins with peace in our individual hearts and minds. It means seeing beauty, harmony and balance somehow, somewhere each day. It begins perhaps with saying, "Today is the best day of my life," and then making it so by living in honesty decency, appreciation, thanksgiving and service.

Want to be part of an epidemic of good? Imagine the word "peace" tattooed on the inside of your eyelids, gazing inward to your very soul, and outward to every soul you meet. Let God's inner smile reach your eyes and lips. Let that smile escape and infect all who see it, with hope, with confidence, with possibility.

Yes. This is about peace...isn't everything when we come right down to it? When one is peace-filled, all is truly well. Thank you Father/Mother God for life, for choice. Thank you Dear One for sharing these moments. You are truly a blessing to the world. Peace be on your heart.

WHAT TO SAY

What to say in the midst of devastation by fire, water and mud, horrendous atrocities, in escalating sadness, for the loss of colleagues, for fellow beings across the world, for friends and neighbors. Courage, that's what; determination, that's what? Faith, that's what. And love, above all, love.

We may be sure that grief will abate eventually, but not before it opens our hearts and minds, strengthens relationships, and promotes deeper appreciation for the majesty and beauty of each moment we spend here as each other in form.

Writes Ernest Holmes, "I know there is a Presence that came with me when I entered this life, and I know that this same Presence will go with me when I leave this physical form, for it is the Presence of Eternal Life, the Life that cannot die."

Does it matter by what name we call this Presence, whether we approach It by science, philosophy or tradition? What matters is that each breaking heart opens wider than ever to seek solace within, love.

Surely we cannot miss the landslide of love pouring forth in labor, service, cooperation, donations of every sort, the cleansing flood of tears, the blessing of inspiration in the face of loss.

Reminds Dr. Margaret Stortz, longtime Science of Mind minister, "No soul is ever lost." Ah, soul. There it is. Along with the flood of memories comes the remembrance of faith: Life is eternal, bodies not so much. Some last a long time, others don't.

The message remains the same: No soul is ever lost. Life, wholeness, Oneness is all there is. And so It is. Hallelujah. You are deeply, truly loved, Dear Heart.

ALL THINGS CONSIDERED

This is about greetings and blessings. When someone asks, by way of a greeting, "How're you doing?"

We could say, "Fine," or "Okay" or "Considering all that's going on, as well as could be expected."

As well as could be expected, considering all that's going on...

Hmmm. Well, no matter what all's going on, let's take a look at how well we can expect to be: Seeing as how we're the perfect children of a perfect God, we could expect to be doing pretty darned well.

We could expect perfect health, knowing there is no illness in God. We could expect to prosper, knowing, as Jesus said, "It is the Father's good pleasure to give (us) the kingdom."

We could expect the unerring judgment of Divine Mind to direct our way. Yes...we could expect to be guided, guarded and protected.

We could expect to be growing daily in wisdom and understanding and in favor with God and man. We could expect to love greatly and to be loved greatly.

We could expect to be enjoying the beauty and preciousness of every moment as our consciousness increases in the awareness of the presence of God, here and now, as us.

Pretty high-sounding stuff...considering all that's going on.

Here's the catch: all that's going on is subject to change as we change our thought about it. That's what's meant by control of conditions. If we're not happy with all that's going on, we can choose to know the omniscient, omnipotent, ever-present Creator knows how to create good, peace, health, abundance, love and joy.

All we have to do is change our thinking to see the possibility, to sense the opportunity—more than sense the opportunity even—to accept the invitation. You remember: Ask and it shall be given unto you, full measure; knock and the door shall be opened; seek and you shall find.

That invitation is just as good to seek ease for a tiny little personal headache, as to seek peace for the family, the country, the planet. The more good we expect, the more good we realize.

There's the promise: Seek ye first the kingdom of God and its righteousness, and all else shall be added unto you.

So...How're you doing?

Fine, thank you, we say, and expecting better and better as our thoughts turn away from limitation of whatever sort toward what we really want to experience: Full, free, glorious Life. The more we expect, the better it gets...the more the glory of God has the opportunity to express. What a blessing...all things considered! Hallelujah! And so It is.

BRASS TACKS and the FAITH SEED

In the middle of the last paragraph on page 59 in *The Science of Mind* textbook is this question: "If we believe that the Spirit, incarnated in us, can demonstrate, shall we be disturbed at what appears to contradict this?"

And our answer might be: My goodness…if we don't believe that the Spirit incarnated in us, the omniscient, omnipotent, omnipresent Creator of the universe, is above and beyond any and all possible limitations we can hatch up or trip into, then we might just as well play ostrich and stick our heads in the sand.

The good news is that even though we have free will, somewhere deep within is imbedded a tiny homing chip beeping at us that there has to be a greater good, that there has to be more to life than lack, limitation and frustration. That's the faith seed, and to protect and nurture it, we can station a sentry at the faith garden entrance…a sentry that recognizes thought weeds no matter how cleverly they are got up.

The fewer thought weeds that get in, the greater growth our faith seed experiences, so that after a while it's big and blooming and un-intimitable. Not only do we let fewer and fewer weedish thoughts into our consciousness, we're at perfect liberty to pull up and throw out those that are already there...those that have been there so long we step over them or around them and don't really notice them anymore.

So, when it comes down to brass tacks* and someone asks, "Do you believe?" You can say, I can say, we can say, "Yes," and really mean it. There is a power for Good in the universe, greater than we are. We can use It, and It can use us.

Whew... that's a relief. Hallelujah!

*Brass tacks? The most fundamental considerations; essentials; realities.

DIS-REMEMBERING

This is about memory and its seemingly capricious facility to hold firmly in place the unpleasant "bad stuff" of the past while toying with the inconsequential goings-on of our everyday lives.

Such as: "Now, where did I put those keys?" "Did I turn off the oven, the lights, the TV?" "What time is that appointment, again?"

It seems more and more folks, more and more of the time are experiencing memory lapses, and it's not necessarily a matter of aging either—which is a relief to many of us. We use pneumonic devices, notes, and classes even, to improve our short-term remembering.

But what do we do about improving our long-term forgetting? I'm not being facetious here…in his letter to the Philippians, the apostle Paul writes in part: "One thing, I do: Forgetting what lies behind, I press on toward the goal…"

Lucky Paul. He says that so easily: "Forgetting what lies behind, I press on…" Perhaps there's more to it; perhaps Paul chose actively to dis-remember.

Dis-remembering may be the key…not to the house or the office, or the car, but to the goal…a richer fuller life.

"Hey, hey, hey," old voices may shout just when life seems to be straightening out and heading in the right direction, "Hey, hey, hey…remember the bad stuff, the hurts, the disappointments, the woes, worries and lacks that always hold you back?"

"Nope," we might reply," We chose to dis-remember such unhealthy stuff long ago."

"Really?"…the voices might continue, "So what's new and startling with you? What's fresh, vibrant, filled with life? What happened to your old grumpy, sickly, bitter self?"

"Oh," we say gently, "We grew up—chose to dis-remember problems, lacks, limitations, injustices. It's like cleaning out the back closet of one's consciousness, throwing out that old pain-ridden out-worn stuff and filling its place with enthusiastic awareness of the wonders and possibilities of NOW."

Dis-remembering—a term coined by an Anglican priest in the prayer booklet *Forward Day by Day*—is consciously, permanently letting go of that which no longer serves, and letting its place be filled with so much good there's no room for less-than-good to return…it's like putting some "how" into one of our favorite truisms: Let go and Let God. Conscious dis-remembering …that's how to let go.

Worth a try, don't you think, Dear Heart? Thank you Father/ Mother God for your patience, your support, your great all-encompassing love. Life is so Good!

Now...what was it I was so upset about?...Ahhh. Like St. Paul, I choose to dis-remember what lies behind, and press on to the goal: a richer, fuller, freer, more peace-filled life. And so It is!

I AM THAT

A wonderful East Indian sage, with a wonderful name, Nisargadatta Maharaj, wrote a wonderful book entitled *I Am That*. It's a thick book, and its message, over and over, is God is all there is:

"There is nothing but Oneness, and I am That…"

No ifs, no ands, no buts.

"I am Life Itself, living Itself as me. I am That."

What a wonderful, clear, pure, powerful thesis…what a guide for living…not quite what some of our modern figures of speech seem to express:

It may not be quite what you were hoping for, but you can live with it; this job is a real snore, but it's a living; I guess I can live with it; you chose it, you live with it.

Yikes! That kind of talk sounds more like putting up with something, making the best of a bad deal, tolerating, sublimating, giving in, than it does like experiencing the vitalizing, energyzing, harmonizing presence of That, the Great I AM Itself, living Itself as us.

When we speak of something we can live with, let's speak with a smile, a glad heart, an open mind, in exhilaration, anticipation, praise and thanksgiving.   Let's live…not just put up with life.   Then we can join Nisargatta Maharaj, and say: Thank God, I, too, am That!   And That's something I can live with.

IDENTITY CRISES

Yours, Mine, Ours, Theirs

Who are we anyway?

Medical science is hard at work dredging the gene pool. Psychiatrists are plumbing depressions, repressions, transgressions and phobias stemming from childhood. Astrologers are taking swings at our todays and tomorrows, based on just when and where we arrived in this life yesterday.

Somebody's bound and determined to let us know who, what and why we are if we don't figure it out for ourselves. We could analyze our risks, lacks, limitations, frailties, bloodlines, etcetera, ad infinitum.

Or we could go Biblical, drink in the sweet nectar of First John, third chapter, second verse, "Beloved now are we the sons of God." And add the metaphysical: There's one Life; that Life is good; that Life is our Life now.

The sons of God, One Life! Isn't that good news! We don't need charts or pills or pedigrees or this kind of car, or that kind of job, or to be any particular age, shape, ethnicity, race, religion or gender. Now is now, and in this moment we are the children, the offspring, the unique expressions of the One Perfect Life, by whatever name we choose to call it. No exceptions.

So much for identity crises. Namaste' Dear Heart. The God in me salutes the God in you, and in all of us. That's ALL of us. And so It is. Hallelujah.

LATCHING ON

Mr. Inbetween, or as some may express it, Mr. Mugwump, refers to the person who sits on the fence with mug on one side and wump on the other. Rest assured, the Mr. is not intended to point the finger at men...in between-ness or mugwump-ness is definitely an equal gender opportunity, and definitely something not to be messed with.

Who says? Hopkins, Emerson, Barker and Holmes in numerous writings throughout their illustrious careers, no doubt. But in this case: Bing Crosby, who sang the following warning near the beginning of his long film career:

"You gotta accent the positive
Eliminate the negative
Latch on to the affirmative
And don't mess Mr. Inbetween."

(The song continues, with biblical reference:)

"To illustrate, my last remark
Jonah in the whale, Noah in the ark
What did they do...just when everything looked so dark?
'Man,' they said:
You gotta accentuate the positive,
Eliminate the negative

Latch on to the affirmative
And don't mess with Mr. Inbetween."

We've probably heard that both Jonah and Noah made it out of their dire circumstances alive...because they put their faith in something greater, more powerful, higher than themselves...and not in something dark, disastrous and lower than themselves.

There's no record of either of them dithering around deciding between Heaven and Hell: "Oh gee...I just don't know what to do. Should I trust there IS a Higher Power...or just give up and go with the flow," and/or, "go down with the ship?"

"No way, Man, look up!
You gotta accentuate the positive
Eliminate the negative
And latch on to the affirmative...!!!"

Dear Heart...that's still the message for you and me and everybody else this moment, no matter what whales or rolling billows we may be facing:

Here's an affirmative we can latch on to:

" I trust, I rest, I live and move and have my being in That which is complete, perfect, Divine, whole and happy....In every thought, in every deed, in every act, I am sustained by an

infinite Power and   guided gently into an increasing good, for myself and for others." *
And so It is. Hallelujah!

*365 Days of Richer Living: 5/9 and 5/10 last lines.

LETNESS, LETNESS, LETNESS

Let us cast the bushels off our candles; set our cities on a hill; grasp Life's chalice by the handles; tip it up and drink our fill. And from that fullness, let us give, give, give.

Out of money? Ahhh, then we have to dig deeper. We've all heard money isn't everything, and, that money doesn't buy happiness. So much for money.

Now, what about happiness, that state of well-being like an inner hum that says, "God's in His Heaven, all's right with the world."

Let's go deeper. God's Heaven is right where I am, where you are, Dear Heart. Money or no money, we can't dislodge the Inner Lodger because It's who we are.

Happiness then, for example, equals not the comforting awareness of money in the bank account, but the thrilling—like a buzzing in the elbows—the thrilling awareness of God/Spirit/Brahma/Allah/Vishnu/Atman within, specifically within, feelably within, continually within…never changing, moving out, abandoning…within.

It's the Inner Bank that never runs dry, never takes a holiday, makes every day a holy day: A whole, complete and perfect day of support, supply, inspiration, healing and delight, if—and here comes the caveat—if we let it.

What a place of power! That's right: good old free will *would* have to rear its ugly head right when we were on a roll. Our beloved Creator gave us the power of free will, the power to choose…and bless our hearts that includes the power to deny Its presence.

"Oh no, there's no God here, no good here. My life sucks. So cut out the cutesy Pollyanna crap…"

Oooh, that's harsh. It's also inhospitable, slamming the door on God, on good, on account of conditions, or heredity, or upbringing, or luck.

But luckily, it doesn't change the Truth: There's One Life, that Life is the Creative Spirit by whatever name; that life is good, and lovingly particularized in, through, and as Its creation: Each and every one of us.

Also luckily, that One Life, by whatever name, is infinitely patient, ready and waiting to burst forth the very moment we open our hearts and minds, our awareness, to even the mere possibility of Its existence.

Letness, letness, letness. Oh my God, I am expressing Thee as me! I am, I am, I am. And so I let it be…and feel those elbows buzz.

Hallelujah.   All is truly, wonderfully, deeply, deeply, deeply well.

LISTEN UP

Isn't it amazing that the Creator, by whatever name, speaks to each of us in ways that speak to each of us.

No matter how many different drummers are being marched to, the heart of each marcher beats to freedom, to life and more life, to wholeness, wellness, Oneness.

Imagine all of us marching to our different drummers, yet marching together, in the same direction: Up; no one condemning, criticizing, coveting or needing to convert anyone else. Acknowledging each other? Yes. Appreciating each other? Yes. Admiring each other? Yes, that too. Unity in diversity.

We have the opportunity to witness this every Olympics…the real competition is one on one…each athlete reaching for his or her personal best. For some that means medals, for others, the satisfaction of just taking part full out.

It's the same for us, Dear Heart, medal or no medal, we're all in this together, living up to the challenges on the ice, the slopes, in the pool, on the track, the moment-to-momentness of being here and now and turning to the Coach in so-called victory or defeat. One on one.

Isn't it amazing that that coach, the Creator of us all, by whatever name, speaks to each of us in ways that speak to each of us. What a concept!

Would it not behoove us to listen?

Summer

SACRED VOWS

We wed ourselves to each other, a career, a cause, a lifestyle, and vow unending allegiance in perfect sincerity. Sometimes those vows hold true...witness golden anniversary celebrants, Oscar winners, Nobel laureates, philanthropists. And that's good.

Yet times change, the world changes, and we change. . That's good too, but what of the vows that fall by the wayside. What then? Ah...that's the time to take a vital first step toward the One thing that doesn't change, that's forever, and underwrites the partners, the career path, the creative breakthroughs, and all else desirable for a happy and satisfying life experience.

That vital step is going first to First Cause, Spirit, Creative Intelligence, God by whatever name. Then, come what may, we truly know where our priorities are, and we start in again...fresh energized, awake and aware, our primary vow of allegiance pledged to That which is ever present within each of us, all-powerful, all-wise, all-loving.

Witness the ordination vows by maturing ministers, pledging themselves to continue in service to Spirit. What a blessing. Let's join them, Dear Heart, going deep within to that from which all blessings flow. And then, let us freely, joyously give thanks. Hallelujah.

FOUR LITTLE WORDS

This is about four little words. But first, a short story: Among the guests at the wedding reception was a little girl, about three years old, wearing a full-skirted, flowered dress and little stiff white sandals. She also wore glasses, evidently to correct whatever was amiss with her here-and-now eyesight...but her insight was perfect.

She couldn't stop dancing—tap, tap, tap—those little stiff shoes made such a captivating sound on the hardwood floor. Swish—her dress swirled around her as she dashed away whenever her tapping was noticed.

But then, she was back: Tap, tap, tapping, and swishing, again and again; eyes beaming shyly through her glasses, apparently oblivious to her parents' reproving glances.

The poet Hafiz, 14th century Sufi mystic, spoke to this very phenomenon:

"Every child has known God. Not the God of names. Not the God of don'ts. Not the God who ever does anything weird. But the God who only knows four words and keeps repeating them, saying, **'Come dance with me.'** Come, dance.

Hafiz also had four little words for us grown-up children:

Plant. So that your own heart will grow.

Love. So God will think, "Ahhh, I got kin in that body! I should start inviting that soul over for coffee and rolls."

Sing. Because that is a food our starving world needs.

Laugh. Because that is the purest sound.

And so It is, Dear Heart…Seven centuries…four words: **Come Dance with Me.** And four more: **Plant, Love, Sing, Laugh.**

In closing, let's add our own four: **Hallelujah. Life is Good!**

(**The Gift,** Poems by Hafiz, the great Sufi Master, pages 270 and 330, translations by Daniel Ladinsky.)

ONWARD AND UPWARD

It's graduation time for many colleges, high schools, junior highs, middle schools, elementary schools, even some kindergartens. Babies are graduating from lolling to crawling, to walking, to talking, to pre-school, and the cycle begins again. Life is all about moving up and moving on from one stage to the next. Definitely worth celebrating.

As Spiritual Beings, we graduate from one stage of awareness to the next as we grow in faith, passing through experiences that challenge us, strengthen us, call on us to call on Spirit within.

We graduate, step by step, from focusing on the material world of possessions and competition, fear and uncertainty, to the realization that we are, in Truth, Spirit in form.

Most of us don't wear cap and gown for these spiritual steps toward greater awareness of Oneness...but maybe we should. How about little stickers of a mortar board and tassel. We could mark each new level with a sticker...on our refrigerator, or the bathroom mirror, or the inside of a cupboard door...somewhere handy for us to see them and be re-minded of how far we've come in faith, in trust, in compassion, in peace and freedom.

When tempted to repeat a grade, or return to a lower level, we could look at our row of stickers and say to ourselves: "I did that already! No need to worry about that again," or, "Hey! Look at this! Remember when I used to think I had to run my life all by myself? That was before I learned to release doubts, let go of fears, and love Life exactly as it is, day by day."

We could get to where each day is a graduation day; we could reach levels of awareness we didn't even know existed. There's no limit to Infinity, and there's no limit to the boundless possibilities of Life as Spiritual Beings.

We could say, and believe: "I am whole and free through God as me. I am well and successful in everything I do. The healing, harmonizing, vitalizing, energizing power of the Holy Spirit permeates every atom of my body, every thought, every emotion, every action, every experience, and I am filled with perfection."*

God is so Good! Hallelujah. Here, have another sticker.

*Dr. Joseph Murphy, *Healing Treatment*, Collected Essays

HAIL, HAIL, THE GANG'S ALL HERE

Excitement! My high school class is having its first reunion in 50 years. It's about time, someone said. It's now or never, someone else added.

But we don't have to wait 50 years, or even 50 minutes, or 50 seconds to hold a personal class reunion. If we are created in the image and likeness of God the Good, than we can start every day in reunion, getting It (Capital I) back together:

Welcome happiness and health; it's always great to see you. Reliability! Wow, I'm glad you're back...where've you been lately? Generosity; thanks, always reminding me to share my share of good.

Forgiveness...and friendliness...welcome home. Service and flexibility...yea...glad to see you. Gosh what a wonderful group: Excellence, creativity, harmony, and detachment! Thank God you're back...I've been missing you for sure. Confidence, kindness....mercy! Someone asked about you just the other day.

And the list goes on and on. And as we call the roll of all the wonders that we are, we embrace our own individual class reunions, our expressions of Life Itself in love, in humility in ever-increasing awareness of who we are and what we are here for.

We are Spirit in form, here to give voice and action to the best that's in us—reunion— Oh my… isn't it great to be alive, to be rich, rich, rich!

Hey! Here comes thankfulness, and close behind…Peace. Praise God, we're all here. Whole, complete and perfect.

And so it is, Dear Heart, Hallelujah!

INSIGHT...HAPPY FATHER'S DAY

This is about insight...looking within to the Source of wisdom, power and love, to that Great I Am in whose image we are made. When we say together, "I am whole and free through God as me..." it means we are throwing ourselves fully into the activities, the requirements and challenges of this moment knowing, and knowing that we know, all is well and life is good.

This knowing and knowing that we know is not some kind of puzzle or tricky languaging. It is acknowledging consciously from the depths of our being that there is a Power in the universe greater that we are. A Power to which there are no impossible tasks, no impenetrable barriers, no unplumbable depths or Incapacitating fears.

And, that Power is acting now, here, as Its beloved you... as Its beloved me. Oh goodness. Oh peace and joy and strength and delight. Oh supply of all that is needed this moment.

Dear Heart, as we turn within, we find ourselves re-minded by the One Great Mind. Life *is* good and very good...this we know and we know that we know. No mystery here. Our conscious awareness of our true nature is amazing, comforting and empowering.

There is no rock so heavy God can't move it. No blossom so beautiful it can't express more beauty. We are one with the Father within; it is the Father within that doeth the works; and what wonderful works they are! Hallelujah. Happy Father's Day!

GRATITUDE

Here it is, The Fourth of July, the traditional day of parades and picnics, and flags flying, of fireworks and dire warnings about flying sparks and furtive terrorists…the perfect day for gratitude, beautiful, profound gratitude.

The Rev. Peter Marshall chaplain of the United States senate more than half a century ago is credited with saying to his wife and children as they stood on the steps of our nation's capitol, "For all that isn't quite right about it, think of all that is."

Think of all that is right about it. Think of all that is right about it. Not only could we apply those words to our country, but to our homes, our families, our work, our spiritual communities, our own secret hearts. Think of all that is right. That little phrase can open the way for gratitude, for joy in small things when big things seem overwhelming…for releasing consciously and purposefully, thoughts, emotions, and feelings of sadness, hurt, lack and limitation…fears that maybe, just maybe, we aren't enough, we don't know enough, we don't have enough.

Gratitude can stop that kind of thinking smack in mid-downward spiral. Gratitude, giving thanks for what we do know, and what we do have, one positive thought at a time, is like plucking cloud after cloud out of our personal sky until guess what…there's the sun!

Yea! There is God, Spirit, Creator… by whatever name, All that is, omniscient, omnipotent and omnipresent. That means that we, being part of The Great Oneness, can stand on the steps of our own experience and say gratefully, "Think of all that is right about it."

And so It is, Dear Heart. Hallelujah! Happy Fourth!

REPORTING FOR DUTY

This is about reporting for duty, based on the theory that if we're still here there's still a need for the job we were sent here to do. Sound a bit far out?

Okay...try this: Imagine waking up each morning and announcing: Reporting for duty! And then expecting the day to unfold with opportunity after opportunity to do that duty.

Call it embracing the Alfred Hjelm model. Alfred Hjelm lived to be a very old gentleman, and in his later years, having passed 90, would awake, look around with a smile and announce to himself—unaware a daughter was keeping a watchful eye and ear on him—"Hey Alf...you're still here. You're back for another great day!"

Was Alf, in his wheelchair with oxygen at hand, in a position to end wars, rescue economies, deliver nations from dictators? No. His job was much more basic, and he did it consistently, one smile, one cheerful word, one instance of patience, of courage, of encouragement...one day at a time.

Alf's job was to change the world for the highest good of all, and his duty station was right where he was. His tools? A loving heart and open mind...God's heart and mind individualized as Alf Hjelm.

So, what do you think, Dear Heart? While we're still here, we might as well report for duty. God's open mind and great sweet loving heart are right where we are right now…this moment. Do we stifle or celebrate, spring into life, or hibernate? What say we give peace, poise and prosperity a go?

Hallelujah…reporting for duty it is! Thank You God.

RERUNS

Ah, reruns: Those old standbys we tuned in to years ago perhaps and have been tuning in to faithfully ever since. We know the dialogue, the action by heart. There's something comforting about the familiar, and maybe this time things will go better.

Egad! It reminds of the definition of insanity as doing the same thing over and over and expecting it to turn out differently.

Do we really need those faithful old stories of lack, limitation and woe? Couldn't we say goodbye to reruns forever? Oh, oh...here comes the commercial:

"There is One Life; that Life is Good; that Life is our Life now. That Life is whole, complete, perfect, new, fresh and vibrant each moment.

"So Friends, it's time to tune in; set our expectations on letting that Life live us more fully than ever before, and for the highest good of all concerned.

"It's time to release the past so there's room to find the good, good, goodness of the present. Act now, don't miss out."

It's a technique highly recommended by Helen Keller, who wrote: "Life is either a daring adventure...or nothing." No reruns for Helen.

Perhaps she was following the advice of Jesus to seek, to knock, to ask and to receive.

Of course, we can stick with reruns. Life takes us at our word, our thought, and says, "Yes, My Dear," no matter what we choose. But, we could spring into action.

We could entertain a new thought, an outrageous one preferably, one that says: Hey, I really do believe there's good for me, and I should have it. If Helen Keller can see the light in spite of seemingly insurmountable obstacles, so can we all.

That thought deserves a super hearty **Hallelujah** don't you think?

FULLNESS

We like our gas tanks to be full; our bank accounts to be full, our cups and glasses and plates, our dance cards, and sometimes even our agendas, to be full. We are urged to be thought-full, mind-full and care-full...to be thank-full and cheer-full.

Fullness is wonderful, depending on what that fullness is of. So, Let our thoughtfulness be of excellence, patience, steadfastness and service; let our mindfulness be of our true nature...freedom for ourselves and others...of reverence for all life; let our carefulness be of tact and justice, orderliness, compassion and respect.

That brings us to thankfulness for life itself, not just the big stuff—those great unchanging Principles of Truth—but the little things too, like seeds coming up and rain coming down, like students, and teachers, looking forward to back to school.

Finally: Cheerfulness. Cheerfulness is sort of like enthusiasm bursting the bounds of its person and spilling out toward others. Not a bad idea, becoming cheerleaders for Life as a life work...surely that's a valid reason for being.

Our role models are kittens and puppies and toddlers, spilling over, bouncing back, nipping and tucking in irrepressible joy…Cheer-full.

And should anyone say, "Uck, you're full of it!" We just smile and nod and say, "Thank you, same to you, and may this delicious moment of summer fill your thoughts with delight, love and peace, too. So there!"

And so It is. Hallelujah!

THE EARLY WARNING SYSTEM

This is a test: Do things happen *to* us, or *for* us?

If *to* us, then we have the opportunity or temptation—some might even say, the obligation—to feel like victims... waaah! Why us! Oh, woe.

If *for* us, we have the opportunity, the challenge even, to take a deeper look and say...hmmm. Why us? What's this all about? What can we learn? How can we grow? What is the healthy, life affirming message here?

Are we going to sit and starve because things aren't going our way? Or, are we going to wade in and create a new way, a more satisfying, life-enhancing way...spit out the pits and be nourished by the Spirit of the thing? Ahhh...the Spirit of the thing, of ALL things, of all that is...Back to Basics!

We each have a helping of Life. It may seem as if some get huge helpings, and some get skimpy little scraps...But, what do we know, really?

Reminds Religious Science founder Dr. Ernest Holmes: "There is no great or small to the God that maketh all."

We can grieve our own personal, national, and international losses, and those brothers and sisters swept away in natural disasters, floods and fires, in wars, uprisings and protests. And we should.

We should throw our hearts open wide, and right along with our hearts, our minds, praying to realize ever more deeply that no life is ever lost, no matter its length, or lack thereof, or the circumstances of its shedding human form…laying the body down.

Life is eternal…something each of us will personally realize sooner or later. In the meantime, we have the opportunity—the obligation, should we choose to accept it—to show forth the best of Life as we know It, expressing the love, the decency, the compassion, the generosity the peacefulness, the wisdom, the discernment and, yes, the joy, in gratitude that we have another day, hour or minute to let the light of Spirit illumine our world for the highest good of all who are still suited up.

And so It is, Dear Heart. Oh my! Hallelujah!

A CALL TO ARMS

Isn't it amazing that we can whinny and cry and allow despair to nip at our heels, and even creep into our conversations. And yet...and yet there's something in us that knows, that leads us to call a friend for support, or put the shoe on the other foot, and offer friendship and support to someone in need.

That something is Life—God—our higher power, the Oneness that binds us all together, that raises us up, that comforts and sustains the hurting Little Us. Underneath always—no matter how low we go—underneath always are the Everlasting Arms, our ever-present help in trouble, no matter how big or how small the trouble may be, devastating or fleeting.

This is not to make light of seemingly horrendous events, situations or conditions.

Oh, yes. Actually it is intended to make light...at least to remind us that the Light is always there, patiently waiting for us to recognize It and invite It into our conscious awareness.

"Spirit recognized must demonstrate," reminds Reverend Dr. Kathianne Lewis of Seattle's Center for Spiritual Living, "Our word spoken, or unspoken in thought, must out picture."

Let it be a picture, then, worth embracing. Let it be filled with love, and peace, with support and inspiration, with respect, delight, and vitality.

Let our word recognize Spirit as all there is, and in everyone. Let our word, our prayer, be for understanding. And while that understanding grows, let us acknowledge that which is greater than our present understanding, greater than our every need, greater than our every hope.

There is One Life. We are here and now in that Life, and in that Life we will ever remain. It races through our individualities expressing the highest and best we can imagine. Onward and upward, Dear One.

Life is good. Watch for that goodness. Wait for that goodness. Know It. Feel It. Share it. Allow It to be so.

And guess what! So It is, thank God, so It is! Hallelujah.

CAPACITY

Says *Richer Living:* "...our inheritance is the capacity to express Life with a punch, a zest and a joy."

Hmm...capacity. When our vehicle fuel tanks run low, we head for the nearest station and fill up to capacity. Whew! That's a relief. Now we can keep going until the next fill-up warning.

Or, if we're leaping into the vanguard of the electric car phenomenon, we head for a plug-in. Whew! That's a relief. Now we can keep going until diminishing capacity again demands recharge.

But hey, who's driving this thing? Do we keep as close an eye on our own inner awareness as we do on our vehicle gauges? Do we take a moment to recharge when conditions and events take us beyond our usual limits?

Do we realize we carry our own Power Source, filling station, plug-in place of unlimited capacity right where we are, no matter where we are?

Do we take a few moments to affirm our connection to all the Power, all the Wisdom, all the Presence there is, with no "empty" signs, no "sorry, out of service" notices, just the sweet vitalizing, deep-down knowing Spirit is always ready, willing and able to take us anywhere we truly wish to go, all the time, day or night…holidays even?

We do? Whew! That's a relief. Hooray for us. We know how to keep going. We know we have unlimited capacity for Life. Punch, zest and joy indeed!

Hallelujah!

DIVE IN

"Are you ready for a miracle?" comes the question. "Ready as I can be," comes the response.

Great! There's still enough sweet summer left to experience the miracle of freedom.

Suppose we've been bouncing on the end of the high dive board long enough. Backing up is hard to do, both physically and ego-wise; going forward still looks scary even though we may have bravely decided it's now or never.

Well, it's NOW, time to take that leap of faith: Bounce…bounce…bounce…Whee! We manage to release fear if only long enough to take off: Swan dive, jackknife, somersault, belly flop even, into the waiting arms of God the Good…the endless pool of possibility.

Oh whee! I'm free: I can do it, whatever it is: Go to school; get back to school; start a job; end a job; heal the bod; heal the relationship, zoom into the new season with reason to rejoice. Choice is made, the Law engaged.

It's the miracle moment when inherent faith and trust thrust us off the end of the board, into greater life, health, harmony…to get in the swim, so to speak. Hooray for us!

Spirit, God by whatever name, is a great coach. Hallelujah!

IMAGININGS

Imagine being so open to peace that all not-peace falls off, having no place to attach.

Imagine being so open to health that all not-health has no chance to gain a foothold.

Imagine being so open to supply, naturally expecting and accepting daily needs and desires being met, that limitation goes wanting for even a hint of recognition.

Imagine being so open to love that one's eyes and ears and heart and mind are filled to overflowing with the delight, the mystery, the wonder of being alive, being aware of that aliveness, surrendering to it so deeply that not-love has no chance to advance.

Imagine a world where illness, fatigue, poverty, fear, greed, need, want, boredom and hopelessness are replaced by enthusiasm, appreciation, curiosity, adventure, abundance and fulfillment.

Imagine being satisfied, just realizing each moment's perfection. Then, the secret smile becomes irrepressible, erupting and spreading from one's face to another, to another, to another until the whole world is alight.

Imagination is a good and powerful thing, God given and God blessed...as are we all. And so It is. Hallelujah.

NEW STATE SNACK

This is about snacking…that's right, snacking. Within the not-too-far removed past came the announcement that one western state had actually named an iconic gelatin dessert as its official snack.

I'm not kidding about this. Supposedly, when the citizens wanted a pick me up, they reached for that jiggly state snack and dug in enthusiastically.

Hmmm. Just suppose we declare our own state snack to be…Spirit…omnipotent, omniscient, omnipresent. Good idea. If we find our state of health a bit peaked, we could snack on Divine energy. If the state of our finances is less than flourishing we could reach within for a snack of realization: It's the Father's good pleasure to give us the kingdom; there's no lack in Infinite Good.

Relationships in a sad state of affairs? Sounds like time for a snack of Divine Love and compassion, a time for snacking on stillness and knowing there's only one relationship, and that's that perfect state of our union with Spirit.

We could beat this metaphor up ad infinitum, but you get the idea…whenever we feel a need, a lack, a desire, we feed that hidden hunger with the knowledge that

God...Spirit...the Creator by whatever name...is right here, right now, in, through and as each of us with all the love, all the power and all the wisdom there is.

All we need to do is ask, believing, and the universe must say, "Yes, my dear." It's the law of Cause and Effect. It doesn't jiggle. It doesn't wiggle. It doesn't melt, and it's not improved with whipped cream or sliced bananas.

Spirit: the snack of a life time. No additives, no preservatives...all natural and instant!

How about a little snack right now? We could take a deep, deep breath...and say: "Oh my God. I am expressing Thee as me, whole and free, and all my needs are met now"

Wow! Hallelujah. In gratitude we let it be.

OH MY GOODNESS

Perhaps its way old fashioned and out of date: You may not be familiar with the expression "out of the goodness of my heart." But I can remember hearing it often as a kid.

One neighbor might say, for the help or the mess of beans or the armful of firewood or whatever, "Thank you, and what do I owe you?"

And the answer would come, "Think nothing of it. It's out of the goodness of my heart."

What a concept. What a beautiful truth. We could do things out of the goodness of our heart day in and day out and never run short. That's because when you come right down to it, our heart is God's heart, inexhaustible, all wise, all powerful, everywhere present all the time, ready and longing to be expressed.

Think for a moment…What might we do— just speculating, not "shoulding"—what might we do today just out of the goodness of our heart? Maybe we could smile indiscriminately, say "hi" to a bird or two, give up a treasured snit, volunteer at the spur of the moment wherever help appears to be needed, etc.

A sneaking suspicion arises that doing things just out of the goodness of our heart leads to greater health and happiness all the way around.   And the thing about sneaking suspicious is that they creep up on you, and WHAM, good happens.   It can't help Itself, thank God.

How wonderfully fortunate we are to know deeper than deep that God is, that God is good, and that moment-by-moment we can express more God just by acting spontaneously out of the goodness of our heart.

READY...SET...PUSH

Suppose we push our spiritual Good Will Button right now, this instant, and it sticks, inducing us to produce only good will from now on...

Good will toward ourselves, toward each other, toward our work, toward our play, toward our country, toward all other countries...good will pouring forth all over everywhere, everyone, everything, all the time...There's nothing we can do about it...even though we might try to focus on worry, doubt, fear, grief or judgment...the button remains stuck in Operation Good Will mode.

Sooner or later, that Good Will would engender the peace, love and harmony we say we value most highly in life. Sooner or later it would remind us we truly believe...not just in theory, but in practice...that there is the One Life, in which we all share, that It is good, whole, perfect, complete and expressing lovingly as us now...this instant, the next, and the next.

Sooner or later we'll be up to our necks in good... sooner... or later?.... hmm... why wait? Definitely, sooner. Right now seems like a good time to push that Good Will button, and, if it doesn't stick in Operation Mode, no problem.

We'll just push it again, and hold it down until it does.

Let's synchronize our thumbs, Dear Heart: One…two…three, and push.There! Good, good, good…I think it's sticking.

Hallelujah!

RISING UP

Today, we might expand the finite us, rising up, over and out of whatever may be keeping us in lack, confusion, sadness, disease and the like, to meet and greet the Infinite us, those unlimited God beings we truly are.

Remember those bumper stickers that asked, "What would Jesus do?"
Well, what *would* Jesus do?

1. Give thanks right off the bat: " Father I give thanks that Thou hearest me."

2. Show faith: "I know that Thou hearest me always."

3.Speak the word: " Lazarus, come forth."

4. Surrender: " Father, into Thy hands I commend my spirit."

We can give thanks, show faith, speak the word, and call forth the rebirth of vitality in any area of our lives...*any* area. We can say, "I surrender to Thee in joy, in relief, and in this moment."

Now is the time to give up trying to squeeze God down to our size. Now is the time to expand our selves up, saying: "I cast all limitation aside to leap up, up into the arms of the Infinite."

Too fancy?   Ok. How about, "I get it: I am expressing Thee as me! Use me to express Thy friendliness, compassion, courage, honesty, joy, health, abundance... all good. I am willing to thrive."

And so It is.

SKIPPING THE STONES

This is about precious stones: millstones and milestones.

Our friend Webster defines millstone as anything that grinds or crushes, or any heavy mental or emotional burden. Milestone is defined as a significant event or point in development. Both are precious and we may cling to them, changing one into the other so cleverly we don't even notice.

We may recall fondly a significant event or point, a milestone, in our development, and then realize how far back that milestone occurred, and how things may have gone to pot since then…

That's when our milestone, no matter how great and wonderful it was, becomes a millstone, a grinding crushing burden around our neck, the fear of not measuring up to the past leading us to make up excuses for not trying now.

Just imagine Meryl Streep turning down a demanding off-beat role lest it not lead to an Oscar nomination, or Richard Sherman refusing to take the field lest he can't match his previous goal line glory…you get the idea.

What to do? First: Give thanks for both stones: They brought us to the place of discernment. Second: Release both stones: The past is gone, the future hinges on our wise use of today.

So… we skip those stones gleefully, right out across the bay of bedlam and watch them bounce once, twice, thrice, and sink. Hallelujah…out of sight, out of mind.

Now we're free to enjoy the next significant point in our development, a new milestone, letting the daily grind, a new millstone, pulverize fear, worry, stress before they become hangers on, leaving our necks unencumbered by conditions and ready to stick out for peace, prosperity, honesty, heath, harmony and unity. Oh my goodness, life is wonderful.

SOAK IT UP

This is an invitation to join me for a revitalizing soak in the Spiritual spa. Now.

All right...here we are, soaking in good...Ahhh...feel it...every system, organ, gland, bone, sinew, muscle, bit and speck of tissue soaking up good; every pore open to good. Arms, hands, legs, feet, torso feeling the thrill of Life, the tingle of vitality.

Here we are, up to the chins in good... and if there are two or three chins, so much the better. Goodness floods our entire being.
What about the head... nose, eyes, ears, scalp? Of course. And the brain...what about the brain? Ah, yes, the brain is so engulfed in good it no longer bothers to intellectualize. Good is. God is. Heart and soul rule, and the ego throws up its hands and swan dives in with a big splash.

Ah, yes. For a quick dip or a leisurely soak, Spiritual spa is where it's at. And where's that? Ho, ho, ho, within, within, within. You knew that was coming, didn't you Dear Heart! And if we allow ourselves to be thus saturated with good is there any way we can keep it from escaping? No, no, no.

Dr. Holmes says: "… this goodness… flows out in every direction, blessing everything it touches…"

And so it does, Dear Heart, and so we enthusiastically let it flow. Thank you Father/Mother God… Life is so Good. Ahhh, so It is.

SOCKS AND UNDERWEAR

"How're you fixed for socks and underwear?"

That's how my Dad used to check in with, or check up on, my two brothers and myself after we were grown up and out on our own. These days, he might say, "What's up?" or "How's it going?"

In any case, he was reminding us he was there for us, caring about us. The "socks and underwear" were his idea of the basics—you've got them, you're in good shape. Ours was a healthy family relationship.

Spiritually-speaking, we're in good shape if we've got healthy relationship with prayer and meditation. In prayer we let God know how it's going, and in meditation, we receive the clear sense that all is well and God is in charge…that Life is good.

Earthly father, Heavenly Father having our interests at heart. Here's what Dr. Holmes has to say in part about the latter: "… A loving presence enfolds me and a security not born of man is mine. Never again will I fear the future, regret the past or be anxious in the present.

"… The Spirit is within me as definite guidance and complete success. I am protected from all evil for Divine Intelligence inspires me to right action. God knows I am successful, healthy and peaceful..."

At the conclusion of his check-in call, my Dad would say, "So long, Kid. Keep your nose clean and your feet dry." Good advice.

Our Heavenly Father might say, "My children, let us not love in word only, but in deed and truth." That's good advice too.

Hallelujah! All is truly well. Peace and harmony to you Dear Heart, and love, love, love.

UN-THUNK

This is about thinking, or not

Yes. This is the day the Lord hath made, and we can rejoice and be glad in it. Starting now, let's dive into the pool of inner peace, cutting swift and clean through the surface layer of flotsam and jetsam, the oil slick of conditions with their swirling false greasy rainbows.

Let's dive deeply, more deeply than ever before. Abandoning thought, we enter the Truth of Being *as* that Truth, beautifully, perfectly, personified as us, leaving ego behind, unmourned.

We rejoice, rejuvenate, realign and then, re-emerge in this here and now world, filled to the brim with increased consciousness of the Divine from which we spring.

But wait! What if on emerging from the peaceful deep we are assailed once again by thoughts of limitation, lack, sorrow, need and ill health or crumby circumstances!

Not to worry. The answer is clear as the crystal purity from which we draw Life Itself. If such thoughts should dare to assail us again, we shall simply leave them un-thunk. And move on.

This is the day the Lord hath made—we will rejoice and be glad in it. Hallelujah, Dear Heart. And so It is.

KANGAROO SPRING SHOES

Ever hear tell of Kangaroo Spring Shoes? They were two springs each, attached to a base that clamped on over the shoes like four-wheeled roller skates used to.

Their wearer could then bound along, and up—leaping nimbly over obstacles on the sidewalk, outdistancing or rising above ordinary mortals. What freedom!

Even though actually owning a pair of Kangaroo Spring Shoes was hopelessly out of the reach of most depression-era youngsters, that dream, that thought was not, and it fuelled many young imaginations with endless possibilities of adventure—Like Superman, leaping tall buildings in a single bound. What freedom!

Ah indeed!   And that freedom, that exhilaration, is still available, ready to be "strapped on" at a moment's notice or, preferably, worn all the time. It's called faith, and it outstrips Kangaroo Spring Shoes all hollow.

Faith: Imagination fueled with the knowledge and understanding that we are all children of the One Creator, spiritual beings having a human experience, able to access the power and the presence of the One Creator with a single thought: I Am Thee as me, and I Am free! Hallelujah. Praise God.

SUMMER...TIME FOR AMNESTY

Isn't it beautiful, wonderful, fragrant, delicious when the sun comes out and the temperature goes up...when it's so obvious that God's in his Heaven and all's right with the earth...no matter what may seem to be amiss at the moment.

In the old-fashioned days of childhood summer, we used to play kick the can or hide and seek, and when the evening grew too dark and mothers were starting to turn on porch lights, we'd know it was time to give up and call in those last super hiders.

"Olly, olly, oxen free... Olly, olly oxen free," we'd call. And from under the porch, or down from the cherry tree would come the stragglers, chuckling that they hadn't been found; that whomever was "It" had had to declare amnesty.

There's a segue here someplace: Maybe that it's time for each of us to call, "Ollly, olly, oxen free" to all those parts of us that have been hiding out...for whatever reason, for however long; to declare amnesty; let bygones be bygones; clean out the closets of our minds and hearts, and welcome the wholeness of us: No sin, no shame, no missed opportunities, no bungled relationships…just lessons learned, examinations passed.

Maybe the childhood "Olly, olly, oxen free" translates as "I am whole and free through God as me…now…this summer moment."

Maybe it's God turning the porch light on, saying, "Get in here, Beloved, where you belong. Spend the summer in harmony, health and wholeness, with me. It's the best game in town."

And so It is! Now THAT's a hallelujah, Dear Heart.

PLAYING THE ACE

This is about, in card-playing parlance, having an ace in the hole or having an ace up one's sleeve—an advantage held in reserve.

That means, no matter how bad, how hopeless, how confusing, how limiting conditions and effects may seem at any particular moment in this here and now world, we have an ace in the hole, ready to play.

That ace is the deep abiding knowledge that there is One Life, One all-pervasive good, One power, One wisdom, One presence and that That is all there is. All. All. All. That means we are inescapably part of that One— the Creator—and the Creator knows what It's up to, and is infinitely capable of healing, supplying, cheering, protecting, comforting us.

Life goes on, whether we lose track of that fact or not. Life continually, wonderfully, blessedly, eternally, is.

Should we forget, or waver, or give in to panic, we might take a look at the trees changing color, dropping leaves in preparation for the next step in their continuum. Closer to home, we could call a friend, or be our own friend and wrap our arms around ourselves in a nice hug and say to our little personality, "Peace, peace be still."

We can, in other words, pull out that hole card. Let's call it the wholeness card. It's there. Never doubt that it's there. Just draw in a deep breath of remembrance. We can even say, should the quavering continue, "Lord I believe. Help Thou my unbelief."

My dad, trying to teach me to play cards with him and my brothers, used to say, "When all else fails, Honey, play the ace."

That's still the best advice there is, whether the game is pinochle or life. The ace, that advantage held in reserve, Dear Heart, is the eternal Presence within each of us as omnipotent, omniscient, omnipresent wholeness…our hole card. So deal 'em up, we're ready.

Fall

GIRDED UP FOR HARVEST

Yikes! Here it is September already, back to school weather, back to cool weather, to longer nights and shorter days. As we move out of summer and into the season of harvest, we realize the true meaning of reaping what we have sown. Those seeds we've been planting in consciousness are reaching maturity, right now.

Now, we're not talking about the woe-is-us stuff, worrying about possible fruitage of fear and lack, chatter thoughts occasioned by temporary fascinations with enthralling media bombardments. No. we've girded up—put on the whole armor of God (must attire for every season). The shrapnel of doom and gloom thoughts just bounces off, leaving a small dent here and there perhaps, but no permanent damage.

As Ernest Holmes would say: "That's nothing. Pay it no mind."

No. We're talking about our ever-growing awareness that God really is all there is. We're talking about our deepening in faith, our coming closer and closer to our true place in the universe, about finally letting go and letting the God, the Good within, out. That's our real harvest: embracing, expressing more good, more God, for our benefit and the benefit of the planet and all of its inhabitants.

This fall is definitely a time for high, wide and handsome harvest celebration. Higher, wider, and much more handsome than ever before. And what a great harvest "handsome" includes: liberal, gracious, generous, suggestive of health and strength, good looking, pleasantly proportioned, graceful.

Yes. Our faith is high, wide, handsome, and then some, for there are no limits to the omnipresent, omniscient and omnipotent Life of all life. That's our life, Dear One, now, and we know it!

So as summer draws to a close, we spring into fall with renewed zest, vigor and confidence that all is God, all is good, all is well.

With grateful hearts we say, Thank you Father/Mother God for the gift of life and the good sense to increase our awareness of life's fullness and wonder, thought by thought, day by day. Hallelujah.

ETERNAL LIFE

It's been 15 years since 9/11/01. Practitioners and congregants began gathering at the Center for Spiritual Living soon after hearing the news that day and for days afterward, sitting in silence, or chanting to soft music, hour after hour.

Reverend Dr. Kathianne gifted those gathering at service with a letter of encouragement, and a copy of Psalm 17 from *A Book of Psalms* by Stephen Mitchell. In the introduction to this small, powerful book, Mitchell says praise is the dominant theme of the greatest of the psalmists...a rapturous praise, a deep, exuberant gratitude for being here.

"The mind in harmony with the way things are sees that this is a good world, that life is good and death is good," says Mitchell, adding that the mind in harmony with the way things are "feels the joy that all creatures express by their very being, and finds its own music in accompanying the universal rapture."

Emerson writes: "Only the finite wracks and suffers, while the Infinite lies stretched in smiling repose."

Praise? Rest? How dare the psalmist praise and the Infinite rest while there's such turmoil and grief here and now...unless, of course, the psalmist knows as the Infinite knows something that may have slipped our minds temporarily: There's One Life, eternal, whole, complete, perfect.

Practitioner Bill DeYoung, mentioned Life going on...in the babies born throughout the world that September 11: innocent, oblivious to what's going on around them, and excited to be here. Excited to be here... celebrating with squawks and gurgles, and yelling at the tops of their little lungs, showing their excitement in their typical baby way... praising life and demanding a full helping.

The young girl who died in the Arizona Gabrielle Giffords shooting incident was a 9/11/2001 baby... bright, eager, filled with love, ambition and the promise of leadership. Did the way she died cancel out the gifts she shared during her nine-plus years here? In Spirit there is no time, no space, only the present moment in which to choose joy or despair.

Deep heartfelt joy is a spiritual victory over terrorism, over doubt and fear...a regeneration of hope, a reaffirmation of faith: Spirit constantly blesses us all to greater awareness and understanding: There *is* One

Life, whole, complete, perfect, and eternal.
Hallelujah, Dear Heart, hallelujah!

SNAPSHOTS (9/11)

Shortly after September 11, 2001, the New York Times began running a special page dedicated day after day to those who perished...little illustrated articles, roughly the same size, whether the subject was the president of a company, or a temporary employee.

As one of the writers phrased it, "Importance is not measured in terms of annual salaries. Instead these are snapshots of a life...each heard the beat of their own drummer, and our aim is to capture that essence of each person."

Well, Beloved, we know what that essence is, don't we: God expressing Itself individually and enthusiastically. As we think of those we know or have known and go for snapshot moments that truly capture each person, we recall moments of rapture, of delight, of satisfaction, of courage, of sharing, of nurturing, of entertaining, of inspiration, of peace, beauty and industry...and on, and on, and on.

We can honor and cherish each of our loved ones, whether or not they are still here in form, by seeing their very best in moments when their truth of being shone through so brightly and vividly, shouting, "Here the Great I Am is!" Snap shots.

And guess what? We can do the same thing for those who, for whatever reasons, are less near and less dear…for deep in our hearts, we know they too are beloved of the Father. Snapshots.

And…guess what again? If we can do that for our loved ones, and for those who challenge us, we can do the same thing for ourselves. We can see the many moments of being and doing our best…don't be skimpy here…and we can know these moments outweigh, outnumber and outshine any little less-than-favorite snapshot moments…even those we may have blown up into wall-sized murals, or had printed on our T-shirts.

As we continue to bless and honor those thousands of saints who died waking us up, we can also bless our loved ones, our not-so-loved ones, our challenging ones…and ourselves.

Snapshots of the heart. God being.

Ahh! That's perfect! Hold it right there…(click, click) Wonderful…snapshots.

UPS AND DOWNS

Up and down…opposite ends of the stick. But if one reverses the stick, up becomes down, and down up. This isn't about mincing words, it's about considering the concepts of highs and lows in life, and how they are, in a way, interchangeable.

When we're experiencing lows, what's the only way to go? Up. Suppose we think of down as the springboard to up. "Down time" is an expression that has come to mean time out…time to rest, reorganize, rejuvenate, get one's self together.

Other people, events, circumstances tend to drag us down we may say. But in truth, don't they really drag us up? The down part is having to face up to some challenge, to grow up, to shape up. Again, isn't down a springboard for up? Don't we build patience and flexibility by dealing with whatever hand we're dealt? When we go down for the count, doesn't that give us the opportunity to get up rather than give up?

Robert Frost wrote a poem about facing challenges as climbing a mountain. One line, loosely remembered, says…after all a small way down isn't so far to one who's come a long way up.

We've all come a long way up in these last few months, a long way toward realizing God is in charge, and giving thanks for that realization...for the growing knowing that the One Life is personal to each of us as we step up to our responsibility to speak our word...as we choose peace, respect, decency, harmony...upness. As we get down off our high horses and love and bless and serve our brothers and sisters the world over.

So, the next time somebody asks, What's up? The answer comes with a smile: I Am, thank God, I Am.

GOD GOT ME HERE

Russell Wilson says it easily, earnestly, often, and first, "God got me here." Then he goes on to talk about his coach, his teammates and his father.

"Why not you, Russell?" his father would say, "Why not you being a pro quarterback?"

Why not indeed. So he learned, he grew, he trusted, he practiced, then learned, grew, trusted and practiced some more. Sure enough, he became a pro football quarterback, one of the youngest ever, and began setting records.

He loves Life, his coach, his team, his family, his town, his job, and he's still learning and growing and trusting and practicing.

The point, Dear One? God got us here too. Why not us living our dreams and loving our coaches, teammates, jobs and families? Why not us expressing our generous helpings of Life to the very best of our abilities, and discovering abilities we didn't even suspect we had?

We've got the formula: learn, grow, trust and practice. It's a lifelong daily routine, keeping in shape, but we can do it.

God got us all here, and God doesn't make mistakes. All in all that'ls good news.

PLAYING THE GAME

Said Ernest Holmes, "I enter into the game of living with joyful anticipation, with spontaneous enthusiasm and with determination to play the game well, and to enjoy it."

Dr. Holmes' words capture the essence of this here and now life as lived by Rev. Jackie Allen, devoted Science of Mind practitioner, minister and teacher.

What is spontaneity but the deep knowledge that Spirit will express, must express and *is* expressing in the moment...though Its particular vehicle, us, may feel tongue-tied and blind-sided.

As Rev. Jackie Allen was wont to teach her many, many practitioner students over the years: speak your word with determination to play the game of life well, and to enjoy it.

"Laser Treatment" Rev. Jackie called it...straight to the point, with all the clarity musterable in the moment...wellness, wholeness, One-ness...and so It is done.

Sure unbelief may get in the way. That's where the determination comes in. "Oh no you don't," we might say to our quavering Little Whiner selves, "Wake up and be thankful you're no longer the victim of conditions...of fear, and doubt, and ignorance...wake up and let your Greater Self run the show."

In other words: Let go and Let God: Trite little slogan, or the wisdom of the universe in just five little words? It's the privilege of each of us to choose.

Rev. Jackie continually made and renewed her choice...entering into the Christness of her being...entering into the game of living with spontaneous enthusiasm, joyful anticipation and the determination to play the game well and to enjoy it. She communicated that spontaneity, joyful anticipation and determination to so many others that they too...that we too...might pass it on. Let go and let God.

RAIN? REIN? REIGN?
HOW'S THAT AGAIN?

When our ears hear a certain homophone we could flash on the rains, that keep falling, piling up, and spilling over until it looks as though we may be heading toward a replay of that Biblical deluge of 40 days and 40 nights: Sogginess.

Or, we could envision the reins, those lines of control and guidance we exert—or not—over our thoughts and actions as we go about our day, reining in that which is unproductive or inappropriate: Pickiness.

Or, we could circumvent precipitation and thought control entirely and go straight to the Presence of God, the peace and harmony, wellness and goodness that reigns, as the all-pervading atmosphere of our experience when we accept deeply as truth that God is all there is, and all is well.

God reigns supreme as our moment to moment confidante, guide and refuge throughout this lifetime and eternity. When It reigns, It pours: Thankfulness.

At this point Dr. Holmes weighs in: "We enter into this divine state of being in such degree as our own thoughts are peaceful, joyous and perfect. To practice the presence of

God is to practice the presence of perfection, of wholeness. This perfection and this wholeness include joy, peace, and the fulfillment of every legitimate desire."

And Dr. Holmes offers us this affirmation: "I have a spiritual vision within me which beholds a perfect universe. Daily this vision guides me to success, happiness, prosperity and physical and mental well-being. My spiritual vision is open—I am awake to the greater possibility."

Notice that Dr. Holmes says nothing about the weather. He does mention keeping our thoughts focused—reined in—and our spiritual vision up, and he recommends living consciously and continuously within, in the realm of the Most High where Truth reigns.

In a way, it's like building an ark as the waters rise, and whistling while we work, remembering no matter what kind of flood may come along, in truth all is God, and all is well. What say, Dear Heart—let the rains come! Hallelujah, hallelujah, hallelujah! And so It is

TRICK OR TREAT

Let's take shameless advantage of a time-honored Halloween activity to segue into a real spiritual treat.

No matter what personas, what costumes we have got ourselves up in, there's one Block where we can count on the perfect sweet treat every time, and that's the One who recognizes us instantly, as Chips off the Old Block...no shame, no blame, no worry, no confusion, no scary stuff, only love...

Metaphorically speaking, the instant we knock, Spirit/God/Wholeness whips open the door and holds out the old mail bag, overflowing with perfectly individualized love notes. I have a hunch yours may be included in this sneak preview:

Dear Chip,

This very moment you are so precious, so loved, so cherished, so delighted in...and guess what? This very moment is the only moment there is...ever! Cheers, God.

Dear Chip,

How do I love thee? Omnisciently, Omnipotently, and Omnipresently. How's that for a vote of confidence? There's no way you can escape, so just say those three little words: I surrender, Dear! Always, God.

Dear Chip,

By saying "Good is all there is" and blessing and praising the good in your life, you add to your good and to that of everyone else. You're a treasure without measure…just couldn't resist a rhyme this time. Love, God.

Dear Chip,

This is a thank you note from ME to you because you have created that place in your heart where you are in constant touch with ME. You are a fantastic individualization of the Great I Am. Sounds pretty impressive, doesn't it? But after all, you are what I Am because I Am ALL there is. What a partnership. Thank you for joining. Love, God. P. S. You *could* tell your friends!

And finally:

Dear Chip,

How wonderful it is to meet you in that inner quiet place, to hold you in my arms (so to speak), to comfort you, strengthen you, open all the doors of wisdom to you, through you. Every time I look at you, I say, "What a good idea creation was after all!" You are me in action every moment, every day. And I'm proud to call you Chip.

I love you, and don't you forget it. That's an order. Yours, God.

And so It is, Dear Heart. Hallelujah. How sweet is that!

THROW THE RASCALS OUT

It's time for policy changes, for ousting dictators and tyrants.

Emmett Fox, philosopher, scientist and Truth teacher, reminds us in his book, *The Sermon on the Mount,* of Jesus' instruction to go into our closet to pray that the Father Who sees in secret will reward us openly with the fruits of our labors. That closet is the secret place of the Most High within our own hearts. The fruits of our labors are the results of our thinking...cause and effect.

If things aren't going as we'd have them go, says Fox, perhaps we need a policy change in our secret place...think rightly within, and sooner or later, all will be well on the outside...nothing has any real significance but a change of policy in our consciousness...our so-called closet.

So, perhaps it's time to oust the tyrants of hatred, guilt, shame, blame, conflict, retribution, fear, unworthiness, envy, and their cohorts. Perhaps it's time to banish for good and all whatever dictators may have kept us in bondage, poisoning our bodies, our relationships, our life experiences.

How? Withdraw support, that's how! Bar the closet door and pay no attention to the poundings, the threats, the whining. Stay firm: Consciously circle up with love, peace, harmony in alignment with right action. Right thinking is allowing our minds to be permeated with thoughts of what we'd really like to experience…not with excuses, not with habitual blockages of time-honored limitations.

Fox reminds that God/Spirit is not confined to time and space. With the Creator It is always now. Should limiting thoughts again arise, now, we have Divine permission to kick them out.

Dear Heart, let's accept freedom from dictators and tyrants of thought now, speak our word of release this moment with thanksgiving, and know in our heart of hearts that it is done. And so It is Hallelujah.

For good measure, a postscript from J. R. Price in *The Workbook for Self Mastery:* "Jesus didn't kid around. When He made a statement, you could bet your life on it."

MURPHY'S LAW

This is about repealing Murphy's Law...or not. You know, Murphy's Law: If anything can go wrong, it will; You can count on it: just watch and you'll see.

Some of the stories about things going from bad to worse are funny, in a rueful sort of way. The German language has a word for it: *schadenfreude*, meaning roughly "too bad happiness," or "Yikes, I'm glad that didn't happen to me, but since it happened to somebody else, it is rather funny."

Now, repealing is serious business and may be time-consuming. We need to take a closer look at Murphy's Law: If anything can go wrong, it will; you can count on it; just watch and you'll see.

What a powerful focus of expectations! Talk about greasing the skids for disaster! Mentally imaging what else could possibly go wrong, in an already completely unfunny situation and... sure enough, it does. Then saying in resignation, well, I guess that's the way things are meant to be.

Oh my goodness...Ah, that's it: Goodness. Poor Old Murphy did not create the universe, and is only one small (albeit beloved) droplet in the vast ocean of creation, not the

Creator Itself, the Omniscient, Omnipotent, Ever-Present help in trouble the psalmist talks about.

We have learned to know and trust that regardless of whatever conditions, circumstances and effects are at hand, Good is happening. We can count on It because creation is always toward greater expression of Life, else It would destroy Itself.

"Life does not destroy, it builds, always in advance of what has gone before," says Judge Thomas Troward, a powerful metaphysical guide for Ernest Holmes..

"There is a power for good in the universe greater than we are, and we can use it," says Dr. Holmes.

"If anything can go wrong, it will," says Murphy.

Hmmm. Repeal might focus too much attention on the negative. Let's just sign Murphy up for Beyond Limits, and turn our attention to the good happening all around us, bolstering the tiniest smile, the smallest kindness, the moment of peace, with more of the same.

Let's go for compassion, for understanding, for flexibility, for love—oh yes, for true, gracious, grateful love. Let us let Spirit flow through us, creating Heaven on earth.

Let us know in our hearts and minds that God is, and then just see what happens. Good happens, that's what. That's a law we can count on. Hallelujah.

WHO'S WHO

I may not know *who* you are by name, Dear Heart, but I know who you are by nature. I know that you are the beloved of God, created in God's image and likeness. I know that you are a spiritual being having a human experience, and I know that human experience can be painful, exasperating, tempting, threatening, terrifying, and sublime. Yes, sublime. That mean lofty, noble, majestic, grand.

Seems like a major contradiction perhaps, but we humans can rise to just such heights when we act from the God Self within.

The challenge, then, is to keep that God Self constantly at the ready. Some call this staying prayed up.

Once we learn the Truth (capital T) that God is all there is, including us, and once we are able to accept that Truth—not only to learn It, but to know It as the real us—then we can call on the Wholeness we know is within to express and to do so appropriately in each now moment.

Perhaps we speak our word for something as simple as patience, as profound as healing for a loved one, as urgent as guidance in an emergency, as basic as food and shelter.

The catch is, we speak our word believing. Believing, Dear One. You have your own personal individual reason for a specific gift or blessing, and you are receiving it this moment because you have spoken your word and taken action, believing. I know this to be true for you: that the Holy Spirit is expressing Its perfection through your physical body and the body of your affairs now.

Feel It. Breathe It. Smile It. Know It. All is truly well. The Lord is in His holy temple, and that temple is right where you are. Hallelujah!

ARMOR UP

You are whoever you are, and I am whoever I am. Yet we have something marvelous in common: We are unique creations of the Holy Spirit, individual waves on the ocean of Life, so to speak.

Before we get too poetic, let's take a look at the every day nitty gritty of being human, which, of course, we also are. Our human selves are under constant media bombardment to beware of threats to our health, our livelihood, our relationships, our peace of mind.

We are advised to take this, not that, to eat this, not that, to smell better, work harder, and enjoy life more. And, most importantly, that enjoyment absolutely depends on protecting ourselves from identity theft.

Identity theft...that's a hot one. We know who we are, individualized expressions of God, and that's something that cannot be stolen. Our God selves are absolutely impervious to conditions and effects. And to make doubly sure, we can, as the Bible advises: Put on the whole armor of God. What do you suppose that armor might be?

How about Truth, ever-flowing, lovingly-overriding negativity.

Truth: There is One Life; that Life is God; that Life is our life now, present every instant in power and wisdom, always greater than any condition or situation we might stumble into.

Yep, that's It: Truth ever-flowing, lovingly overriding negativity. To be short and sweet about it, let's just slip into the whole armor of God: Spiritual Teflon. Ahhh...perfect fit. Hallelujah!

BARNACLES

This is about barnacles. Yes. Barnacles are marine crustaceans that attach themselves, firmly, to ship bottoms...much like certain ideas, thoughts and feelings attach themselves, firmly, to our subconscious minds.

Just imagine, Dear Heart, if you were a ship, how good it would feel to have the barnacles scraped off your hull. No questions about how they got there, or how long they've been there... just the relief of having them gone! Ahhh... free at last... ready for smooth sailing.

Now... about those barnacle-like thoughts that have attached themselves, firmly, to our consciousness over the years. Scraping? Yikes, that's hurtful, yet we sometimes resort to guilt, shame, withdrawal, lamentations of woe and unworthiness, and complaining, until— instead of those thought barnacles—we scrape off friends and family who finally grow weary of hearing about our pain and suffering.

Barnacles of bad belief are not relieved by whining and declining. No outside scraping, scrapping or carping can help. For us, Dear Heart, you, me, and everyone else, it's an inside job. Proven barnacle relief is at hand this very moment, right here, right now... within.

There's no need for scraping, just press the inner release button and let Spirit flow.

Speaking your word may go something like this: Desist, dissolve and disappear all accumulated limiting thought. I release you, known and unknown. I let go of you stultifying thought-barnacles, and let God within fill my mind with thoughts of love, peace, health, harmony, abundance and joy.

Now, breathe a sigh of relief as the healing flood of Life is unleashed. Aaaah. Free at last. Yes. Free at last...ready for smooth sailing.

God is so Good. Life is so Fine. Ahhhh...and so It is. Hallelujah.

BLESSINGS, BLESSINGS, BLESSINGS

Count your blessings, says an old hymn, *name them one by one, and it will surprise you what the Lord has done.*

When upon life's billows you are tempest tossed, when you are discouraged thinking all is lost, count your many blessings, every doubt will fly, and you will be singing as the days go by.

It seems the older we get, the faster days do go by. So it becomes more and more important that they don't fly by unnoticed and/or unappreciated.

At a friend's suggestion I began jotting down a few lines each night before bed about what had happened that day, so I wouldn't get caught up in thinking nothing ever happened.

As I paid attention, the jottings took longer and longer and the few lines became many because there's no such thing as nothing happening. Life is happening 24/7 and the closer we pay attention, the sweeter it is. Many folks keep gratitude journals just to capture, savor and re-savor that sweetness, to count their blessings.

How about breath for number one. Without it we' be launched out of this world into our next experience. Then there are people, and countless opportunities to help, appreciate, learn and love. In each major category there are seemingly limitless variations—blessings, blessings, blessings when we take time to take note.

All ways of saying: There's One Life, that Life is God, by whatever name; that Life is good; that Life is your life, my life, all life, now. And that Life is happening 24/7. Hallelujah!

CALMLY PRAY and RECEIVE

This is about CPR...you know, cardio pulmonary resuscitation.

But wait! There's more to us than a physical body operating in a physical world. We are spiritual beings, created in the image and likeness of God. To be as God intends us to be—whole, free, radiantly healthy, happy and abundantly supplied and nurtured—we may need to practice spiritual CPR...Calmly Pray and Receive.

Calmly Pray: Let our human minds absorb the Truth of the One Mind, seeing the perfection God sees. Then, with grateful hearts, Receive the blessings of peace and love, courage and discernment, putting to rights anything seemingly amiss.

CPR, spiritual and physical, is not a one-shot deal. It needs to be practiced mindfully, continuously, until life—full, fresh and free—is restored. Calmly Pray and Receive. Calmly Pray and Receive. Calmly Pray and Receive. There is One Life. That Life is God's Life. That Life is all there is.

That Life is our life now. Dear Heart, yours and mine and everyone else's. Let us Calmly Pray and Receive It full measure...

pressed down and flowing over...leaving no room for doubt or fear.

The Lord is our shepherd, our guide, our restorer. All is well. Hallelujah.

CROWD CONTROL

This is about dealing with those unproductive thoughts that sometimes crowd into our consciousness as we go about our days and nights.

Of course, you and I know there is no such thing as an unproductive thought, but we seek to choose those that produce peace and harmony, and reject those that produce conflict, confusion and frustration. Many of the latter may deal with what Ernest Holmes calls disagreeable people.

Dr. Holmes agrees that it may be easy to go through life feeling we are the victims of others' thoughts and actions, but he reminds us that Jesus had to deal with disagreeable and unkind people too, and Jesus understood that those people needed love and understanding more even than others.

We are practicing Jesus' teachings, Dr. Holmes says, when we realize that all that needs correction is our own thought. He adds that the seemingly troublesome person's words and actions fail to register in our consciousness when our minds are sustained in a spiritual concept of what that other person really is: God is in the so-called enemy; God's life is his or her life, too, and God's mind is his or her mind.

Next, Dr. Holmes offers an affirmation that includes the following:

"…I do not have an enemy, I have only God's people in my world. No one is vicious, mean or unkind to me for my consciousness cannot receive such wrong ideas. I believe (men and women) are dividualizations of God, and as such, the people in my world are good, loving and kind. No one can hurt me but myself, and I refuse to do that. I keep my thoughts worthy of the Infinite Thinker that is expressing through me. I believe in the Christ in my fellow men and women, and I see them as they truly are."

So, Dear Heart, let us let those affirmative thoughts crowd out any conflicting ones in our consciousness, that we may go through our days in peaceful activity, and our nights in peaceful slumber. Praise God. Praise God. Praise God.

365 Days of Richer Living, p. 293

ENJOY YOUR DAY

As she handed me my groceries and receipt, the young checker looked me right in the eyes and said, "Enjoy your day."

Not, have a good day, or even, have a great day, or thank you for shopping here, but "Enjoy your day."

What an empowering phrase. Those three little words implied both responsibility and possession. Yes, it was my day; it belonged to me, and I was responsible for putting joy into it, for making it joyful. Hmmm. How can I en-joy my day? Tough question!

Really? Then try these: Who am I; why am I here; what is life all about? Oh, I know those answers: I am an individualized expression of Spirit in form, here to express the presence, the power and the wisdom of the Creator Itself…the wonder, peace, harmony, creativity, abundance, joy…

Ah ha! So enjoyment means accepting my oneness with Spirit. No matter what conditions are swirling around, I can dive through all that surface flotsam and jetsam of daily living straight into the depths of Spirit, to be refreshed, renewed, rededicated.

I can remember there is One Life that is good and very good and that Life is my life now.

Conditions come and go, but that Truth remains: There is nothing but God Itself expressing eminently capably as this thing called me.

That's the rock on which I stand, and I can imbue my day with that awareness, blessing all the conditions and effects that remind me who I am and what I'm here for. In short, I can en-joy my day. And what's true for one is true for all. Hallelujah.

GETTING OUT OF THE WAY

We' d hardly think of trying to hold back an avalanche, or a speeding freight train, or an emergency vehicle, or a couple of pro football teams in mid play, or a raging torrent or any other overwhelming power heading straight for us. We'd use our common sense and get out of the way.

Where then, do we get the colossal nerve to stand directly in the way of the source of ALL power, the One Power, Spirit/God, and declare "Oh no, not me," following it up with our particular choice of the following: I'm too old; too young; too inexperienced; to set in my ways; not the right size, shape, color, ethnicity; not educated enough; too educated, not lovable. I know MY limits; no Magic Thinking for me.

Yikes!

Here's what Joel Goldsmith, author of *The Infinite Way*, has to say about that:

"Once we give up concern for this human sense of self and realize that we exist as God fulfilling Itself in an individual way, and that the responsibility is on (God), we relinquish this false sense of responsibility. Then God fulfills Its destiny as individual being.

"To the world it may appear that we are healthy, happy, successful or prosperous; but we know better. Only God is healthy, happy, successful or prosperous, and the good the world beholds is God fulfilling Itself as our destiny—when we stand aside and permit It to do so."

Ah, Dear One, standing aside for God sounds like a plan. How about you and me stepping nimbly out of our own way, letting go and letting God flow through every bit of that conscious awareness we call us.

Oh boy, here It comes now, and we declare ourselves powerless to stop It! Hallelujah!

JOB DESCRIPTIOIN

I once worked in a dormitory kitchen with a young woman who had embroidered across the top border of her white, chef's apron, "Remember Who You Are and What You Are Here For."

That was more than 50 years ago, and those words still haunt me...Remember Who You Are and What You Are Here For.

Well, who are we? Religious Science teaches that we are individualized expressions of God. Since God/Spirit is all there is, and nothing exists outside of God, there's nothing else we could be. Yea! That is indeed encouraging.

Now, what are we here for? How about, to express God in thought, word and deed? As one popular spiritual song puts it, to Love, Serve, and Remember. Okay.

To Love. Yes. To pass on the love that we are permanently tapped into once we accept the basic Truth of our Oneness with God and Man.

To Serve. Yes. To express the virtues of God, those spiritual qualities valued through the ages by all major religious philosophies: Compassion, kindness, respect, honesty, idealism, creativity, patience, service, to name just a few.

And, to Remember. Perhaps that means to re-member our lives, putting back into Divine Order anything seemingly amiss, accepting our underlying perfection, and the longing of God to express through Its us as vibrant health, abundant supply, Divine guidance and direction, peace of mind and right action.

Love, serve, and remember who we are and what we are here for. Yesterday is gone, tomorrow is cooling its heels in the wings. But today, ah today, Beloved. This moment, _now_.

God's life is our life now. Let's not let it go begging for expression, but jump right in with smiles on our faces, gratitude in our hearts, and delight in the opportunities blossoming around us this moment. Opportunities for forgiveness? Yes. Mercy? Yes. Cooperation? Yes. Courage? Of course! Tact? Why not! And courtesy, courtesy, courtesy.

What a grand and glorious day this is, Dear One. Let us enjoy it…_and_ let It enjoy us. Thank you sweet Spirit. Hallelujah.

HUGS

This is about experiencing the loving arms of God.

We may forget occasionally that God, Spirit, the One Life, includes not only the Law: "As a man thinketh in his heart, so he is"…cause and effect. But the Love, the compassionate tenderness of the Beloved toward the beloved: "God so loved the world that He sent His only begotten son"…and we are that son…the Christ in us.

Recalled the witness of an accident in which a car was swept off a mountain pass by an avalanche: "It seems God wrapped his arms not only around the car, but around the four people inside. All were saved."

Sacred readings challenge us to remember that God has two arms with which to enfold us here in our human experience: the arm of justice, and the arm of love.

Of course we're speaking metaphorically, not seeing God as a white-bearded superhuman-like being in the clouds of heaven. But the infinite wonder of Spirit, Essence, The Creator, can and does draw us unto Itself in loving embrace.

Just as surely as we calm ourselves to stillness and drop deeply within saying, "I am whole and free through God as me," we are refreshed, renewed, encouraged, literally wrapped in the Power, the Presence, the Wisdom, of Love Itself.

We're learning that The Law is inexorable: Cause and effect. Let us also keep in mind that The Love is inexhaustible, always there to pick us up and dust us off. Why do you suppose we came up with hugs? Whose idea was that?

Can the individual expression of the One in each one of us cradle its little ego-personality partner, in deed as if in loving arms?

Yes my Dear. Thank God It is so, and so It is!

SAFETY NET

High wire artists, aerialists, are at the peak of performance—and daring—when they fly from trapeze to trapeze, from take-off to landing, depending on their skill and expertise to spare them the embarrassment of falling into the safety net...and think of those who totally defy gravity, and work without a net.

Chances are you aren't a high wire artist, and neither am I. So, what does this have to do with us?

Simple: We can get so caught up in the conditions and effects, the demands and stresses of everyday life we may feel we're walking a tightrope, a high wire, trying to keep our balance, do our work, meet our responsibilities, safeguard our health, and, of course, remember that we are spiritual beings having a human experience!

That's the key! We _are_ spiritual beings having a human experience, and thus we have the safety net of God's love, peace, supply and Divine direction. All we need do is ask, accept, let go of whatever condition or event has us momentarily paralyzed...and drop deep, deep, deep within.

To sum things up:

I pry my fingers of resistance off the trapeze of conditions, and drop into the safety net of God's love...always available, always inviting, no embarrassment needed.

That's God's safety net...feel free to drop in any time! Hallelujah! Isn't Life fantastic!

SHORT, SWEET, POWERFULL

Here's a message of power from Ernest Holmes, written as though it's being directed specifically to you and me Dear Heart. So do take it personally. From September 8, *365 Days of Richer Living*:

"Today you are to hold your thoughts steadfast in the realization that God withholds nothing from you. Therefore, prepare yourself for a life of joy, love, happiness and well-being. Say:

"I believe in myself because I believe in God. I accept life fully, completely, without reservation, holding to the conviction that good is the eternal Reality, that God is the everlasting Presence, that Christ within me is the eternal Guide, that my life is complete today."

No reservations! Did you hear that part Dear One? Isn't it wonderful to realize there are no reservations needed to walk with God, talk with God, call on God any time, any place, for any reason.

We are at home in God...God is at home in us. This fabulous relationship is ours now, and in the continuing moment of now... no reservations needed, ever. All is truly well. Hallelujah, hallelujah, hallelujah! And so It is.

HALLELUJAH ANY HOW

This is the day the Lord has made. Let us rejoice and be glad in it.

What better way to honor this day and the Life that is living us than to stand up or sit up straight, take a deep, holy breath, and, with the exhale abandon ourselves completely to Good. Good, Good, Good...thought, word and deed.

The Reverend Jesse Jennings of Creative Life Spiritual Center in Houston, Texas, shares this short and powerful affirmation for doing just that:

"Today I make my choices from the standpoint of love, releasing the need to condemn the actions of others, removing myself from the role of victim. I celebrate my own positive use of a creative law, knowing that infinite good is unfolding in my life."

And for Good measure: A little Southern Gospel Hallelujah chorus recalled by Shirley Killion (rhymes with million) with love and spunk:

Hallelujah, Any How!
Hallelujah, Any How!
When life's troubles come your way
Hold your head up high and say,
"Hallelujah, Any How!"

MORE GOOD, PLEASE

We've shared the line: Dear God, thank you for all the good you have given me, and please give me more....but...more where, more when, more what? Is this about greed? Surely not.

Here's what Ernest Holmes has to say in *Richer Living*: "...Since God is Infinite, our expansion is progressive and eternal. No matter how much good we experience today, the Infinite has more in store for us tomorrow. We should look forward to this expansion with enthusiastic anticipation. The march of life is not a funeral dirge, but a song of triumph."

Ah...expand the finite—that's us. Open up so there's more room for God, for good: Praise, bless, open, stretch. More, more, more...a new idea, a new thought, new awareness, new possibilities. Sounds good.

Dr. Holmes, offers six affirmations to get us moving confidently and promptly into more-ness:

One: The good that I experienced yesterday is going to be multiplied today.

Two: I cast this good upon every wind of heaven, knowing that it goes out to bless.

Three: I condition my mind to accept greater good for myself and others.

Four: I wait calmly, but with joy, for new experiences to come to me, for new opportunities for service.

Five: I expect my mind to be flooded with new ideas.

And, for dessert, Number Six: I know that the Spirit of the Lord is with me and that the glory of the Lord is around me.

Ah, Dear Heart, what more needs to be said? God is; Good is; We are. In thanksgiving we say Hallelujah. And once more: Hallelujah.

NO TIME OFF

As individualized centers for spiritual living ourselves, let's ponder for a moment what a wonder that is: God the Great, the Good, the Spirit, Power and Presence of Life Itself is right where we are, right now and always.

There's no time off for good behavior, no time outs for bad behavior, no vacations, no days off, no sick days, no coming in late or going home early, no leaves of absence, and no considerations gained by daylight savings time or the reverse thereof. We might take advantage of any of these from time to time, but God…never: 24/7, 24/7, 24/7!

We are never alone, never on our own, never away from the Magnificent Source of Being because It is us; We are of It. By whatever name we may call ourselves, or be called, we are centers for spiritual living…Spirit centered in and living as us.

Oh, aren't we lucky that God is kind, generous, abundant, wise, and all-forgiving…and…here's the really great part: God **is** kind, generous, abundant, wise and all-forgiving, and knows us to be the same.

Dear One, we are so blessed to be the children of love; to have within us the Source of

All Good, the Cause of every effect, the answer to every dilemma.

We are so blessed to be aware that we can turn within at any moment, and say, Oh, my God, I am expressing Thee as me, and I give up even trying to pretend otherwise any longer. I accept, honor and respect this Being I find myself to be, and I look at all other beings with new heart, knowing they too are centers for spiritual living. No exceptions.

That's the good news. All is God. All is good. And we can surrender into that Allness, that Goodness with grateful hearts and peaceful minds, now, as we vault forward into a new day, a new experience of richer living.

GIVING THANKS

The Bible reports Jesus at Lazarus' tomb saying, "Father I give thanks that Thou hearest me, and I know that Thou hearest me always...Lazarus, come forth!"

Some protested: Lazarus has been dead for days, surely he stinketh. Yet Jesus proceeded to speak the words of Life...preceded as always by the words of thanks, speaking from a grateful heart, knowing the wisdom and power are always present, that it is the Father's good pleasure to give us the kingdom...in this case, restoring Lazarus.

But that was ages ago...what does it have to do with us? How can we give thanks when current conditions in our life may seem life-less, yea...stinketh?

We might start by honoring the supposition that God is no capricious dummy, cruel trickster or harsh taskmaster. We might recall former times when things looked just as out of whack. Those times passed and, sure enough, we learned, we grew, we passed out of the tomb of darkness to see the value in what had seemed hopeless.

Why then, should this set of circumstances, personally, nationally, universally be any more difficult, dire, or disastrous? Is God still up to the task of expressing peace, love, harmony, right action, compassion, courage, patience, forgiveness, supply, support, all good? Yes, yes, yes...exactly in as much as each of us lets those qualities flow...uncensored through our thoughts and actions.

How wonderful to know there is a power for Good in the universe, and It can use us.

Father, we too give thanks that Thou hearest us this moment and always. And so it is.

'TIS THE SEASON FOR COOPERATION

At this season of the year especially we give thanks for life, for health, for daily bread and for all the individual blessings in between. We forget about minor gripes and dissatisfactions, overlook annoyances, look deeper into others, seeing why we really love them, and find ourselves giving up the need to nitpick and complain. One upmanship goes down for the count.

At this season of the year especially, we tend to let bygones be bygones, let compassion triumph over prejudice, let sharing and generosity overcome selfishness. Hey! What's happening here? What's going on?

It's simple really: When we loosen our grip on littleness and allow our larger nature to emerge, we become more as God intended us to be...more Godlike.

It's true: A Religious Science mantra goes like this: There is one Life, that Life is God, that Life is good, that Life is our Life now.

That's where the cooperation is coming in. We are becoming more susceptible to standing aside in deference to our better nature. Deference...that means respectful yielding. For example, instead of wasting precious time fretting about what possible seasonal ills such as influenza might befall us, we are yielding to the influence of Good becoming.

That doesn't mean we're becoming goody-goody or doormat-like, it means we're becoming more aware of our capacity to filter our own thoughts and behaviors, truly allowing those that are for the highest good of all concerned to express.

This holiday season, our dearly beloved personalities are respectfully receiving larger and larger—larger than ever—helpings of humanity, humility, divinity, charity and love.

As that little light of yours and this little light of mine burn together and combine…cooperate…with all the other little lights, Good happens…God happens. Limitations lessen as Spirit shines, and hearts are inspired to rejoice.

Cooperation is a good thing, a very good thing, Dear Heart. Let us respectfully yield to it at every opportunity until it sweeps the neighborhood…Heck, why think small!…until it sweeps the planet…'tis the season and we are jolly well thankful, thankful, thankful for it. Thank you, Dear Heart; thank you Father/Mother God, thank you Oneness.

REAL THANKSGIVING

This is about thanksgiving. Not the turkey/cranberry sauce Thanksgiving coming right up, but real 24/7 thanksgiving.

Look at it this way: We made it through the time switch; we made it through Halloween, and we made it through the elections. There's three good reasons to give thanks right there.

"In all things give thanks," says the Bible. Why do you suppose that is? Life is happening all around and through us, and It knows what It's doing. Life is good. It assumes that we want to experience good. It assumes we want what we ask for. Notice that when we focus our thoughts on grief, on lack, on frustration, or...Heaven forbid...on jealousy or anger, we seem to get more of that very thing?

The Bible also says, "As a man thinketh in his heart, so he is." So let's permanently give up thinking downer thoughts. Let's think thanks thoughts for living in a country where playing with time is a big deal, where children put on costumes and go around shouting, "Boo!", where we get to vote for those of us we think will make good leaders. Let's give thanks for waking up in the morning, for having something to eat, and a way to earn a living.

We're not giving thanks that we have blessings others don't. We know God doesn't play favorites. We're thankful that we've waked up enough to know that we truly are all ONE. We know that every time we praise Life, we praise it for all. And, we shall "praise and raise" each other until the balance tips and all are fed and clothed and free.

We give thanks for all the wonderful differences between people, realizing that God loves each one of us greatly, and is standing by to fulfill our word. Therefore, let us let that word be of increasing awareness, of appreciation, of understanding, of delight, of freedom. Let us let words of thanks replace words of worry, or grumpiness, or pettiness.

Let us see Life for what it truly is, an awesome gift…bearing in mind that the Creator Itself has infinite patience, and that sooner or later Good triumphs. Let's vote for "sooner," and as the song says, "Thank God for being God today."

Hallelujah. So It is, Dear Heart. So It is.

HIGH NOTE

Let me hear that high note Maestro! Fill my heart with ecstasy, my eyes with beauty, my ears with harmony. Let all my faculties revel in the Truth of Being, that One Life that is All there is, here and now.

And bless the here and now that was there then, that planted the seeds of peace and plenty now bursting into bloom. And, may I plant, this day, more of those same seeds, and, in the continuing moment of now, more seeds, so that all may partake, and in turn plant, that there may be a tsunami of love engulfing the planet.

From Ernest Holmes, " I am now inviting the Spirit within me to flood my mind with its wholeness, to bring warmth and color and feeling and love into everything I do, say and think. I believe at the very center of my being there is the (person) whom God has made, a perfect (person). Therefore I lay aside all fear, all doubt, all misunderstanding, all uncertainty. I know that Life has need of me or it would not have put me here."

Ahhh…short and sweet. What a wonderful vision; what a wonderful life we all share. What more is there to say except thank you, thank you, thank you God. Hallelujah!

HOLY, HOLY, HOLY

O Holy Night, O holy day, oh holy moment, when born in us is the deeper, truer knowledge that we are, indeed, Spirit in form...the beloved of the Father.

Amid the last minute rush of errands and activities, of observing holiday traditions of many cultures and faiths, working, shopping, cooking, inviting and being invited, we know deep down that Christmas is about the birth and rebirth of Christ consciousness within. Ever more clearly it becomes evident that there's no room in the inns of materialism and holiday hoopla...

The only room that counts is the humble welcoming manger of our own hearts. There the light shines, the love glows, from there the contagious joy escapes to bless the world...people of all faiths...our brothers and sisters in Spirit...One Life in God...Unity.

Says Ernest Holmes: "I make of my mind a stable and welcome the Christ idea of perfect spiritual man. I give the gifts of my attention, my love and my substance to this idea born within me. I am open to the Divine...I let God be born into my thinking and feeling.

"I share this birth to a higher understanding with all men everywhere. I revere the memory of Jesus and let his teachings be in me a light unto my world, and others seeing my good works shall find the Light of Truth within themselves. (Christmas) is the day of Christ, the day of Truth, the day of birth into a greater Good."

So…stars, shepherds, sheep, seraphim and sages…once again bringing the message: Wake up, Wake up! Love God, live God, let God live you. Hallelujah my friend. Happiest holy days.

BAH HUMBUG

The story of Ebenezer Scrooge and his Christmas journey from miserly grinch to kind, loving benefactor dramatically illustrates the power of changing thinking and changing life.

Scrooge gets some help from three ghosts—the past, the present and the future—and wakes up to goodness just in time to really be of service to his fellow persons.

Each of us has a past which has helped shape who we are today. We can greet that ghostly past and its characters with compassion and understanding, or remain stuck with its pain, disappointments, loss of innocence.

Each of us has a present...the gift of Life here and now... and the constant choice to give thanks for it and expend it in service for our fulfillment and the highest good of all concerned, or whine about limitation.

And each of us knows each present moment builds toward the next, setting the tone for how our future experience will be...one ghost, one thought, one choice after another.

One choice might be to echo Scrooge's nephew Fred Honeywell, who being gruffly bah-humbugged, says, "Christmas a humbug, Uncle? You don't mean that, I'm sure. I have always thought of Christmas time, when it comes round, apart from the veneration due its sacred name and origin, as a good time, a kind, forgiving, charitable pleasant time; the only time I know of in the long calendar of the year when men and women seem by one consent to open their shut up hearts freely... And therefore Uncle, though it has never put a scrap of gold or silver in my pocket, I believe that (Christmas) has done me good, and will do me good, and I say, 'God bless it'."

Bob Cratchit, Scrooge's "clark", chooses to acknowledge the nephew's outburst with a vigorous clapping, and Scrooge—as yet to be visited by the ghosts—shouts another "bah humbug," and threatens Cratchit with loss of his situation.

Then come the ghosts, convincing Scrooge to choose Life for himself and others, to make every new moment come alive with loving kindness.

Our choices may not result in our immortalization in English literature, but they most certainly may lead to happier, healthier, more abundant, more satisfying, more worthwhile life experience for ourselves and others...All others.

SUPPOSE FOR A MOMENT

Suppose for a moment that you are a Divine gift—the perfect expression of the Living Spirit in here-and-now form. Suppose for a moment that within you are love and wisdom and health and abundance, courage and discernment and joy. The list could go on and on, for the good of God, the Creator by whatever name, is unlimited and ever-present.

This is the day the Lord has made, and you and I are here to see the beauty, hear the music, sing, smile, share, and in so doing serve the Highest Cause by bringing new, fresh moments of peace into our every thought and action, to every place we are and everyone we meet.

Suppose we set the dial of our consciousness to Oneness, Wholeness, Divine Action, and then abandon all efforts to control anything…just let the good flow to us and from us.

We might find ourselves saying in wonder at the recognition, "Oh my God, I am Thee as me, and in this moment I accept myself just as I am, for I am Thy gift of love, of cheer, of generosity, of compassion.

"I get it! I finally get it! And there's no way I can   escape the Truth of my Divine Being. No matter which way I turn, there You are, saying, 'This is my beloved one in whom I am well pleased…in whom I am well pleased, and don't you forget it, or ever again pretend otherwise.'"

And so It is, Dear One, the perfect time to open this day full out…one moment after another. Hallelujah!

YES, YES, YES

Perhaps this is the time for some serious conversation: Imagine you really...truly...deep in your deepest heart, believed that there is only One Life, that you are part of It and that It is ALL of you.

Suppose you believed in the goodness of this Life, and that you, as part of It, were beloved, cherished, and absolutely provided for. Suppose you believed that your health, every bit and speck and atom of your physical body was created perfect and cannot escape that perfection, and that anything seemingly amiss is put right instantly as you relax and say the magic words.

What are the magic words? Ah...there are lots of them, starting with Yes, Yes, Yes.

Or, if that seems too complicated, you could just say: "I give Up."

That's Up with a capital U, meaning: Hey, enough's enough. I can't hold out any longer; I'd rather accept the inevitable now; admit that I am a spiritual being having a human experience, and all that I need is within me.

Ah...all that I need is within me...all health, abundance, right action, all peace and harmony. Yes, yes, yes.

And then, more magic words: Let It flow! Buoy me up! Live me! I pry my fingers of resistance off the trapeze of conditions and fall with a grateful sigh of relief into the safety net of God's perfect presence, power and wisdom. Yes, yes, yes.

To quote Ernest Holmes: "I am aware that God recognizes me as the divine person He intended me to be and I accept my inheritance of wholeness today—now as a matter of fact—why wait."

And more from Dr. Holmes: "I am at home in the universe wherever I may be...one with God, one with people, one with that abiding faith that knows no fear."

There. That ought to do it! Breathe. Yes. Yes. Yes.

CHOOSING THE TOP BRAND

Hello Dear Heart, Happy Old Year! Thank you for showing up this moment that we may kiss this old year goodbye together. Soon it'll be the new year—a brand new year and a brand new playing field.

Let us be sure that that brand is Spirit, and let us clear the playing field this moment so that we are refreshed, and rededicated to express Truth full out.

No doubt we made a similar affirmation at the start of last year. Our hearts and minds were focused on Spirit...and we did the best we could. We came through older, wiser, clearer than ever on just what happiness and wholeness mean in Life as us.

Therefore, whether or not the material conditions and effects of this old year rate plusses, minuses or an intriguing combination of both, it was a good year which has transported us here to the brink of renewed possibility, challenge, reward, discovery and...and...this is the BIG one: Letness.

Yes, letness. You remember: Let go and Let God. Isn't it amazing that we actually have the power to stymie the Universe just by giving our egos another shot at running the show.

Surprise! It hasn't worked yet: Our egos mean well, but they're slow learners and we're moving on to the gifted class, saying "yes" to the Gifts of God. Jesus put it clearly when he said, "It is not me but the Father within that doeth the works."

So our resolve for the new year might go something like this: I let go and let God live me, be me for the highest good of all concerned.

And the default position? There is no way my Little Whiner self can gum up the works, this moment or ever. I give Spirit full reign—Thankfully.

Oh boy…here It comes!

Hallelujah.

Epilog

THE DIVINE SPARKLE

See It. Feel It. Be It.
It's revealing Itself everywhere,
All the time,
Awaiting recognition,
Promising delight,
Hollering in the Silence:
"Let me out! Let me in!
"Let's work. Let's play!
"Let's let this day be filled
With Its promise exposed for the glory It is!"
Gee whiz!
That Divine Sparkle is really something,
Or is It really no thing?
Or All things?
Smile at a baby, and when the baby smiles
back,
You're in.
The baby still remembers Who it is and what it
is here for.
You think you've forgotten…until now.
It's Life—the Divine Sparkle.
Smile at a baby, and when the baby smiles
back,
Or the geranium blooms, or the tomato ripens,
or the bird sings,
You're in!
Welcome home, Sweet Heart,
Enjoy your day.

THE GONG SONG

Overlapping layers of lovely
Reverberating rhymes of sound
abound, abate, then almost disappear.
Almost, because they're here,
Of all places,
As smiles on our faces.
Life is so good.
All is well…hell*
All is GREAT!
Namaste'

IN WORDS OF (MOSTLY) ONE SYLLABLE

Yesterday is not tomorrow
Unless we make it so today.
Love,
Girt**

*Early Science of Mind lore recalls an *almost* impatient
Ernest Holmes responding to a still-doubtful student,
"Oh hell, you're well!"

**Short for Girtabouttheloinswithtruth, God's constant
companion. It's biblical. Look it up.

PSSST...BUDDY, TRY ONE OF THESE

Finally, here's a word from Our Sponsor by two of the greatest copywriters in all of New Thought, colleagues Ernest Holmes and Raymond Charles Barker.

Here It is: "The Spirit within me refreshes me daily."

If that hit the spot, there's plenty more where that came from. You'll find them all together in a bright green volume titled *365 Days of Richer Living*. Better than vitamins; better even than exercise, unless, of course, your exercise includes daily doses of vitalizing, harmonizing, energyzing thinking, inspired spiritual practice.

Short on time? No problem. Grab a one-liner with your toast and juice, or your latte, or power shake or whatever. *Richer Living* is a veritable treasure trove of one-liners.

But this isn't a sales pitch, it's an introduction, deja vu, so to speak. Care for another sample?

"Freed of worry and filled with faith, I have a heavenly experience today."

How about another?

"The more I know of God, the less I can create or experience difficulties."

And another:

"I evolve out of all pettiness into all tolerance."

Goodness! It's hard to stop with just one, or two, or three, isn't it?
That's a rhetorical question. Blessings, blessings, blessings.

Prayer and Practitioners

The object is to be consciously aware of God/Spirit operating in, through and as oneself: I am expressing Thee as me! This is the soul beat, keeping one going just as the physical heart beat keeps the physical body functioning. We can feel our physical pulse. In the stillness we can sense the pulse of Spirit: "This is my beloved in whom I Am well pleased."

Once realizing Who and What we are, the conscious decision is made to let It happen, let God happen, let Good happen. Says Ernest Holmes in *The Science of Mind*, "The one who attempts to heal himself or another through a recognition of the creative power of Mind and the ever-availability of God, is a mental or spiritual practitioner ... He should declare that the Spirit within him is God, quickening into right action everything he touches, bringing the best out of all his experiences, and forever guiding and sustaining."

Dr. Holmes continues, "The layman hopes this is true, the professional practitioner knows it's true, and acts accordingly."

Catching the hem of Knowing's garment for even a nano-second is where miracles come in: Flashes of Truth overriding anything…everything…on the plane of conditions and effects. Miraculous healings: Realizing the true body is the God body, whole, complete and, perfect.

Perhaps this is what Dr. Holmes meant when he said during the dedication of the Whittier (CA) church, "The veil is thin between," and then, "I see it."

Being a practitioner is taking the veil, working it until it becomes thin, thin, thinner, and falls away.

We're powerful enough to thwart our own good. (I'm sure The Creator has been dressed down more than once for giving "them" free will.) What good to us is All-Good if we don't send our little egos out to play and let Spirit have Its way with us. Let go and let God: Timeless wisdom in five little words.

Now, the purpose of prayer: To stay alive, to phone home, to return to sender. Each of us has the inborn sense that we're not alone. We may ignore it, deny it, avoid it, but it's there. Again Dr. Holmes: "The premise on which all mental work is based is perfect God, perfect man, perfect being." Inherently, we believe in and long to express that perfection.

If and let are two very big words in Religious Science. If there is one Life, and if that Life is whole, complete, perfect, good and all there is, then it would behoove us to let that Life flow unhampered through Its crowning creation...us.

Un-hampering is what practitioners do; un-hampering is what clients seek. Introduction to All-ness is the captivating invitation of the Religious Science philosophy. For professional practitioners, the introduction is not enough. They hunger, literally sometimes, for a closer, more intimate relationship.

Others, who sample the introduction and find it intriguing, but daunting, may seek out professional practitioners: "Wow, how wonderful it must be to have the kind of faith practitioners have They can help me, thank God!"

Practitioners came to the party the same way, then moved from "they can help me" to "I can help myself." Next came helping others as the neophyte practitioners moved up the ladder one step, one service, one class after another into complete enthusiasm, the fullness of God, overflowing in expression for the highest good of all concerned.

And so It is.

ABOUT THE AUTHOR

Anne Bock was introduced to the Science of Mind philosophy in 1970 and went on to become a licensed Religious Science Practitioner emeritus at the Seattle Center for Spiritual Living (one of the many Centers for Spiritual Living across the country), where she taught classes, and continues to serve, presenting the Saturday messages on the center's call-in Inspiration Line (206 525 GIFT). She received her BA in journalism and K-12 teaching certificate from the University of Washington, worked on newspapers in Fort Collins, Gunnison and Delta (CO), taught journalism and a variety of language classes at Sequoia Junior High in the Kent (WA) School District. (Cover design and photography by Bob Calkins)